The Pocket Guide to
Every Child Matters

The Pocket Guide to Every Child Matters provides an at-a-glance overview and insight into *Every Child Matters* (ECM) for busy trainees, newly qualified and experienced teachers, support staff and other Children's Workforce practitioners working directly with pupils in primary and secondary phase educational settings.

Coverage includes:

- the concept, aims, principles and policy of *ECM* and its influence on practice;
- how to develop an ethos for *ECM*;
- how to embed the *ECM* outcomes across the curriculum and in personalised learning approaches;
- how to monitor and evaluate the impact of *ECM* at classroom level;
- how to develop effective team work for *ECM* to support pupils' well-being.

The Pocket Guide to Every Child Matters is an invaluable, no-nonsense, user-friendly resource with photocopiable materials, practical tips and guidance on effective strategies, helpful checklists and signposting to further information and resources.

Rita Cheminais is a School Improvement Partner and a Freelance Education Consultant with Every Child Matters (ECM) solutions. She has written a number of valuable books in the area. These include *Every Child Matters: A New Role for SENCOs*, *Every Child Matters: A Practical Guide for Teachers*, *Every Child Matters: A Practical Guide for Teaching Assistants* and *Engaging Pupil Voice to Ensure that Every Child Matters*.

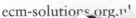

Rita can be contacted at admin@ecm-solutions.org.uk and www. ecm-solutions.org.u[1]

The Pocket Guide to *Every Child Matters*

An at-a-glance overview for the busy teacher

RITA CHEMINAIS

Routledge
Taylor & Francis Group

LONDON AND NEW YORK

First published 2010
by Routledge
2 Park Square, Milton Park, Abingdon, Oxon OX14 4RN

Simultaneously published in the USA and Canada
by Routledge
270 Madison Ave, New York, NY 10016

Routledge is an imprint of the Taylor & Francis Group, an informa business

© 2010 Rita Cheminais

Typeset in Sabon by Wearset Ltd, Boldon, Tyne and Wear
Printed and bound in Great Britain by CPI Antony Rowe, Chippenham, Wiltshire

British Library Cataloguing in Publication Data
A catalogue record for this book is available from the British Library

Library of Congress Cataloging in Publication Data
Cheminais, Rita.
The pocket guide to Every Child Matters : an at-the-glance overview for the busy
teacher / Rita Cheminais.
p. cm.
Includes bibliographical references and index.
1. Children with social disabilities–Education–Great Britain–Handbooks, manuals,
etc. 2. Children with social disabilities–Services for–Great Britain–Handbooks,
manuals, etc. 3. Educational equalization–Great Britain–Handbooks, manuals, etc.
4. Educational accountability–Great Britain–Handbooks, manuals, etc. I. Title.
LC4091.G7C54 2009
379.2'60941–dc22   2009000263

ISBN10: 0-415-47916-9 (hbk)
ISBN10: 0-415-47917-7 (pbk)
ISBN10: 0-203-87496-X (ebk)

ISBN13: 978-0-415-47916-5 (hbk)
ISBN13: 978-0-415-47917-2 (pbk)
ISBN13: 978-0-203-87496-7 (ebk)

Contents

Figures, tables and boxes

Figures

Tables

Boxes

Acknowledgements

My thanks go to colleagues and friends around the country who I have had the pleasure to meet and work with in a number of local authorities, who have encouraged me to produce this introductory guide to *Every Child Matters* for trainee, newly qualified, returning and experienced practitioners in schools and other educational settings, who are working directly with children and young people in classrooms.

Special thanks go to: my late mother, for taking a great interest in my work, and following the progress of my writing of this book while she was alive; the dedicated, dynamic and innovative headteachers' throughout the UK, who have helped me to identify good practice in implementing *Every Child Matters* in reality, within schools; Philip Eastwood, AST for Initial Teacher Training at St Mary's and St Paul's CE Primary School in Knowsley, who keeps me up-to-date with developments in teacher training; all the professionals from higher education institutions and educational publishing who have promoted and referred to my work; last, but not least, Dr Monika Lee, my Commissioning Editor with Routledge, for her valuable guidance throughout the writing of this book, and all the other staff at Routledge who have made this book a reality.

Abbreviations

AfL	assessment for learning
AST	Advanced Skills Teacher
BESD	behavioural, emotional and social difficulties
CAF	Common Assessment Framework
CAMHS	Child and Adolescent Mental Health Services
CPD	continuing professional development
DCSF	Department for Children, Schools and Families
DfES	Department for Education and Skills
DH	Department of Health
DOB	date of birth
ECM	*Every Child Matters*
EP	educational psychologist
ES	extended school
EWO	education welfare officer
FE	further education
GSCC	General Social Care Council
GTC	General Teaching Council
HE	higher education
ICT	information and communications technology
INSET	in-service education and training
IT	information technology
NCSL	National College for School Leadership
NFER	National Foundation for Educational Research
NMC	Nursing and Midwifery Council
NOS	National Occupational Standards
NSF	National Service Framework
Ofsted	Office for Standards in Education, Children's Services and Skills
PE	physical education

PRU	Pupil Referral Unit
PSHE	Personal, Social and Health Education
QCA	Qualifications and Curriculum Authority
QTS	Qualified Teacher Status
RE	religious education
SEAL	social and emotional aspects of learning
SEF	self-evaluation form
SEN	special educational needs
SENCO	special educational needs coordinator
SIP	school improvement partner
TA	teaching assistant
TAC	team around the child
TDA	Training and Development Agency for Schools
UK	United Kingdom
UNCRC	United Nations Convention on the Rights of the Child
UPN	unique pupil number
YOT	Youth Offending Team

Introduction

The government's *Every Child Matters* (ECM) initiative, and the subsequent Children Act 2004, originated as a response to the tragic death of Victoria Climbié and the many other children in England and Wales who are at risk of, or die as a result of, abuse or neglect. The *Every Child Matters: Change for Children* programme may also have been influenced by a similar initiative in the United States, referred to as *No Child Left Behind*, which aimed to close the pupil achievement gap between white, black and Hispanic groups of children and young people.

Since the publication of the government's Green Paper *Every Child Matters* in September 2003, there has been variable progress made towards implementing this important agenda in schools.

Six years on from the introduction of this Green Paper, children's workforce practitioners in schools, which include trainee, newly qualified and experienced teachers, still require guidance and information on how they can ensure they improve the five outcomes for the children and young people they work directly with in schools and classrooms. The implication for children's workforce practitioners working with children and young people is that they need to adopt a holistic approach when identifying and removing barriers to learning and well-being, i.e. focusing on the whole child and young person's well-being, in addition to their learning. Learning cannot take place effectively if a child or young person does not feel safe or when health problems create barriers to their learning. In addition, learning does not take place in isolation from children and young people's feelings; being emotionally literate is just as important.

This introductory guide on *Every Child Matters* is aimed at enabling aspiring and practising teachers, and other practitioners working directly with children and young people in schools and other educational settings, to:

- understand the origin, concept, aims and principles of the *ECM* agenda, and relate it to their everyday work with children and young people;
- know how to develop and promote a positive *ECM* culture, vision and values;
- be able to implement the *ECM* initiative and improve the *ECM* outcomes for pupils they teach, support and work with;
- know how to evaluate the impact of teaching and additional provision on improving the five *ECM* outcomes;
- understand and know how to work effectively and collaboratively with practitioners from external agencies.

Although the book is aimed primarily at trainee and newly qualified teachers, as well as teaching assistants, it is also appropriate for any trainee and newly qualified front-line practitioner from health, social care, education and other voluntary and community organisations who are working directly with children and young people in schools and other educational settings.

The book brings together in one concise volume the best practice gained from schools implementing *Every Child Matters*, as well as some of the most useful information from the author's previous *ECM* publications. It is designed to provide an invaluable resource for busy practitioners, offering useful tips, tools and practical advice on *Every Child Matters*. It can also be used to:

- act as a point of reference;
- inform best practice in improving the *ECM* well-being outcomes for children and young people;
- enable pages to be photocopied for professional-development purposes within the purchasing institution or service.

This pocket guide matters to every trainee and qualified children's workforce practitioner, because it will enable them to focus more on what they do and the impact that their teaching, support and additional provision/interventions have on improving *ECM* outcomes for children and young people.

1

What is *Every Child Matters* about?

This chapter will cover:

- the concept, principles and aims of *Every Child Matters*;
- the opportunities and challenges that *Every Child Matters* offers;
- recent research findings on how schools are implementing the *ECM* agenda.

The concept of *Every Child Matters*

The concept of *Every Child Matters* is to protect, nurture and improve the life chances of children and young people, in particular those of vulnerable children. A holistic approach is recommended, whereby a child's well-being, in addition to their learning, is considered. *Every Child Matters* is about improving the life chances of all children and young people, from birth to 19, reducing inequalities and helping them to achieve better outcomes.

The principles of *Every Child Matters*

Ten principles underpin the government's *Every Child Matters: Change for Children* initiative:

1. Children and young people to fulfil their optimum potential.
2. Early intervention and prevention through improved service provision.
3. Safeguarding and protecting children from harm, neglect and poverty.
4. A well-trained, skilled, knowledgeable and flexible children's workforce.

5. Improving information sharing between agencies.
6. Better-coordinated joined-up integrated front-line services.
7. Greater accountability – impact of provision on outcomes for children and young people.
8. Children to voice their views and inform decision making in relation to personalised services and personalised learning.
9. Safer communities providing recreational and voluntary activities for children and young people to participate in.
10. Improved access to advice, information and services for parents, carers and families on positive parenting, family learning, childcare, adoption and fostering.

The aims of *Every Child Matters*

The overall aim of the government is to ensure that every child and young person has the chance to fulfil their potential by reducing levels of educational failure, ill health, substance misuse, teenage pregnancy, abuse and neglect, crime and anti-social behaviour among children and young people. The government's aim is for every child, whatever their background or circumstances, to have the support they need to:

* *be healthy*: enjoying good physical and mental health and having a healthy lifestyle.
* *be safe*: being protected from harm and abuse.
* *enjoy and achieve*: getting the most out of life and developing the skills for adulthood.
* *make a positive contribution*: being involved with the community and society and not engaging in anti-social or offending behaviour.
* *achieve economic well-being*: not being prevented by economic disadvantage from achieving their full potential in life.

Table 1.1 provides an overview of the *ECM* outcomes. The five *ECM* outcomes are interdependent and show the important link between well-being and educational achievement. They were identified by children and young people during consultation.

Table 1.1 *Every Child Matters* outcomes for children and young people

ECM outcome	ECM aims	Ofsted evidence
Be healthy	• Physically healthy • Mentally and emotionally healthy • Sexually healthy • Healthy lifestyles • Choose not to take illegal drugs • Parents, carers and families promote healthy choices	• Regular exercise taken, including two hours PE, sport per week • Make informed healthy lifestyle choices • Understand sexual health risks, the dangers of smoking and substance abuse • Eat and drink healthily • Recognise the signs of personal stress and develop strategies to manage it
Stay safe	• Safe from maltreatment, neglect, violence and sexual exploitation • Safe from accidental injury and death • Safe from bullying and discrimination • Safe from crime and anti-social behaviour in and out of school • Have security, stability and are cared for • Parents, carers and families provide a safe home and stability	• Display concern for others and refrain from intimidating and anti-social behaviour • Feel safe from bullying and discrimination • Feel confident to report bullying and racist incidents • Act responsibly in high-risk situations • Physical activities undertaken in an orderly and sensible manner

Table 1.1 (*Continued*)

ECM outcome	ECM aims	Ofsted evidence
Enjoy and achieve	• Ready for school • Attend and enjoy school • Achieve stretching national educational standards at primary school • Achieve personal and social development and enjoy recreation • Achieve stretching national educational standards at secondary school • Parents, carers and families support learning	• Have positive attitudes to education • Behave well • Have a good school attendance record • Enjoy their learning very much • Good personal development evidenced by high self-esteem • High aspirations and increasing independence • Make good progress in their learning
Make a positive contribution	• Engage in decision-making and support the community and environment • Engage in law-abiding and positive behaviour in and out of school • Develop positive relationships and choose not to bully and discriminate • Develop self-confidence and successfully deal with significant life changes and challenges • Develop enterprising behaviour • Parents, carers and families promote positive behaviour	• Understand their legal and civil rights and responsibilities • Show social responsibility and refrain from bullying and discrimination • Able to express their views at school and are confident their views and 'voice' will be heard • Involved in school and community activities

Table 1.1 (*Continued*)

Achieve economic well-being	• Engage in further education, employment or training on leaving school • Ready for employment • Live in decent homes and sustainable communities • Access to transport and material goods • Live in households free from low income • Parents, carers and families are supported to be economically active	• Develop basic skills in literacy, numeracy and ICT • Develop their self-confidence and team-working skills • Become enterprising, and able to handle change in their lives • Take initiative and calculate risk when making decisions • Become financially literate and gain an understanding of business and the economy and of their career options • Develop knowledge and skills when they are older, related to workplace situations

The opportunities and challenges of *Every Child Matters*

The opportunities that *ECM* offers to classroom practitioners are:

- meeting the needs of the whole child: their well-being and learning;
- teaching pupils how to learn and acquire the tools for learning;
- teaching pupils how to look after and improve their well-being;
- promoting emotional intelligence in the classroom and whole school;
- enabling pupils to develop into responsible citizens;
- promoting and supporting pupil voice;
- encouraging pupil self-review and assessment of their own learning and well-being;
- personalising learning and tailoring teaching to meet the needs of pupils;
- improving pupils' access to learning by the use of ICT and multimedia technology;
- signposting pupils to appropriate personalised services and extended school activities;
- increasing collaborative working with a range of multi-agency practitioners to share information, knowledge, skills and expertise;
- workforce remodelling which offers new roles to some staff, e.g. Director/Manager for *ECM*; Lead Professional for Personalised Learning; Lead Professional for Pupil Well-being; Coordinator for Multi-agency working.

The challenges that *Every Child Matters* offers to classroom practitioners are:

- an increased focus on the impact of teaching, additional provision and interventions on improving pupils' *ECM* outcomes.
- a greater commitment to parents/carers and pupils' empowerment and rights;
- increased partnership working with a wider range of external practitioners;

- knowing and understanding the different roles and responsibilities of external practitioners and partners;
- having sufficient time to implement and embed *Every Child Matters* in everyday practice;
- promoting greater community participation and cohesion;
- understanding of and familiarisation with *ECM* processes and procedures, e.g. Common Assessment Framework, National Service Framework, Team Around the Child, ContactPoint;
- ensuring effective two-way communication between school staff and external practitioners working directly with pupils in school;
- managing competing priorities, strategies and initiatives within the same amount of time.

Recent research on how schools are implementing *Every Child Matters*

From 2006 onwards there has been ongoing research into how schools are implementing the *ECM* agenda. The National Foundation for Educational Research (NFER), General Teaching Council (GTC), the Training and Development Agency for Schools (TDA) and the National College for School Leadership (NCSL) have published their findings, which focus on some key issues. Tables 1.2 to 1.4 summarise the main findings.

Table 1.2 NFER annual survey of trends in education 2006 and 2007

Changes in schools as a result of implementing Every Child Matters
<ul><li>School improvement plan reflecting the five *ECM* outcomes</li><li>Review of curriculum and current school practice to incorporate *ECM*</li><li>Review of staffing and recruitment for *ECM*</li><li>Increased partnership involvement and information sharing</li><li>Increased extended school work</li><li>Improved school meals and greater awareness of healthy eating and healthy lifestyles.</li></ul>
Challenges schools face in delivering the Every Child Matters *agenda*
<ul><li>Sustainability of funding and human resources</li><li>Having sufficient time to develop and implement *ECM* whole-school</li><li>Developing closer collaboration with other services and agencies involved in supporting children and young people's well-being.</li></ul>

Source: Chamberlain *et al.* 2006; Lewis *et al.* 2007.

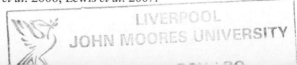

Box 1.1 What teachers want to help them implement the *Every Child Matters* initiative

The GTC highlighted the need for:

- Sufficient well-trained, high-quality front-line practitioners from services and agencies to respond effectively to the *ECM* agenda in order to deliver preventative interventions.
- Greater opportunities for more inter-professional learning, training and development between school staff and multi-agency practitioners in order to improve integrated working.
- Inter-professional training in using inter-agency frameworks and protocols, e.g. National Service Framework (NSF), Common Assessment Framework (CAF), ContactPoint, Team Around the Child (TAC).
- Clearer and improved information for schools on where to refer children and who to seek specific expertise from.
- More up-to-date information about voluntary sector provision available.
- More information and a clearer understanding about the expertise, role, procedures and processes of children's services and agencies working with schools.
- More information about the role of the local authority Children's Trusts.
- Greater sharing of exemplification of good practice in how to implement *ECM* and develop effective multi-agency partnership working in educational settings.
- More support needed in monitoring and evaluating the impact of additional provision and interventions on improving *ECM* outcomes.

Source: GTC 2007a.

Box 1.2 What school leaders want to help them implement the
Every Child Matters initiative

The report findings confirmed the need for:

- Greater clarity of purpose in connection with other agencies.
- Schools establishing and consolidating links with partners and other agencies.
- Schools creating a shared vision, purpose, goals with other agencies.
- A common understanding of the professional language used across different multi-professional disciplines.
- Schools establishing a clear line of communication, accountability and decision making with other agencies.
- Greater involvement of outside agencies on the school's leadership team.
- Whole school staff training on strategies for fostering multi-agency ways of working together.
- Shared evaluative feedback existing between schools and multi-agencies for *ECM*.
- A clear understanding of the respective roles and responsibilities of partners and agencies involved in improving *ECM* outcomes.
- Sufficient local authority support to secure multi-agency inputs for schools.
- Designated staff in schools with sufficient time to coordinate multi-agency partnerships for *ECM*.

Source: Harris *et al.* 2007.

Questions for reflection

- Having read the three research report summaries on *Every Child Matters* in schools, where is your educational setting in terms of implementing *ECM* whole school?
- What next steps does your educational setting need to take in order to improve the implementation of *Every Child Matters*?
- What opportunities and challenges does *Every Child Matters* offer to you in your current role?
- Who will you share this information about the implementation of *Every Child Matters* with in your educational setting, and why?
- As a result of reading this first chapter, how do you intend to use and apply the information to your own current practice?
- What changes for *Every Child Matters* do you wish to see happening in your educational setting as a result of your dissemination of the information gained from reading this chapter?

2

Developing a vision and values for *Every Child Matters*

This chapter will cover:
- establishing a shared vision and values for *Every Child Matters*;
- the features of a positive *ECM* culture in a school/setting;
- understanding change for *Every Child Matters*;
- managing change for *Every Child Matters* in a school/setting.

Developing the vision and values for *Every Child Matters*

Developing the fundamental values, guiding beliefs, vision, culture and sentiments existing among a group of people or within an institution is important in relation to *Every Child Matters*.

Every Child Matters is an initiative that pervades every aspect of school life. It is important to weave the *ECM* principles into the daily life of the school, both in the formal curriculum and through a clear and consistent strong school value of care.

A good starting point for developing a vision and values for *Every Child Matters* is to collectively, as a whole school/setting, respond to the following, in order to agree upon a shared vision and belief for *ECM*.

- In my school/setting *Every Child Matters* means...
- The vision and beliefs for *Every Child Matters* in my school/setting are...
- We are an *ECM*-friendly school/setting because...

- The views of key stakeholders about *Every Child Matters* in my school/setting are...
- The ethos for *Every Child Matters* in my school/setting is...
- The school/setting could be even more *ECM*-friendly if it...

The visioning for *Every Child Matters* engages stakeholders in thinking about where they want their school/setting to be in three to five years' time in relation to *ECM*. A mind map can be produced collectively, to express this longer-term vision for *Every Child Matters*. Figure 2.1 is an example.

Where stakeholders may be having difficulty agreeing upon a vision for *Every Child Matters*, the following statements can be utilised to promote discussion and to reach a final decision:

- The well-being of all pupils is just as important as their learning.
- The well-being of all our pupils is of paramount importance.
- The five *ECM* outcomes underpin whole-school policy and practice.
- Every child matters in this school/setting.
- Everyone matters in this school's/setting's learning community.
- *Every Child Matters* is crucial to enabling every pupil to reach their full potential.

The top 20 features of a positive *ECM* culture

1. Displays in the main entrance, around school and in classrooms depict examples of pupils achieving the *ECM* outcomes.
2. Photographs of staff, governors and members of the school council reflect diversity and indicate key roles.
3. Pupil voice is given a high priority, and is reflected in the Charter for Children.
4. Parents, visitors and practitioners from external agencies are made to feel welcome, and their contributions valued.
5. The school/setting includes the full diversity of learners.
6. A Key Worker system is in place for pupils.
7. There is equal opportunity and accessibility to the curriculum and extended school activities/services.
8. The staff are flexible and responsive, working successfully as a team to address pupils' learning and *ECM* well-being.

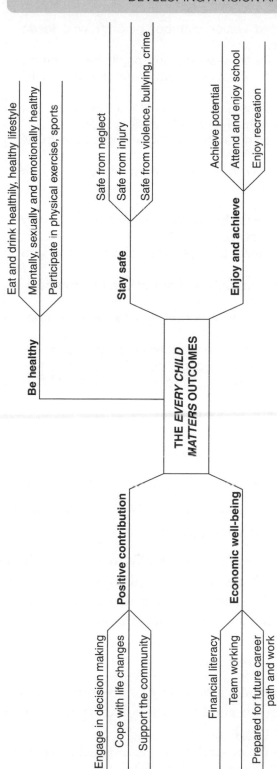

Figure 2.1 *Every Child Matters* mind map.

9. There is a designated senior member of staff who leads *Every Child Matters*.
10. Multi-agency practitioners working with pupils have time to meet school staff to discuss impact and review *ECM* progress.
11. Effective two-way communication exists between school and parents/carers, school and multi-agency staff.
12. There is regular, ongoing staff training linked to the *ECM* outcomes.
13. Planning for *Every Child Matters* is informed by the needs and views of pupils.
14. The views of parents/carers are valued by practitioners.
15. Transition arrangements for pupils in relation to *Every Child Matters* are effective.
16. Good proactive links exist between the school/setting and the community.
17. A range of facilities and activities are offered to the community.
18. There is a calm, stress-free, emotionally intelligent environment.
19. Standards of pupil behaviour and attendance are good.
20. The most recent Ofsted inspection report judged achievements to be good/outstanding, in relation to the *ECM* outcomes.

The above top 20 *ECM* ethos features provides a useful checklist.

The importance of the *Every Child Matters: Change for Children* initiative

Ofsted has found that schools offering healthy food options have better outcomes, and that schools with extended services have better standards. Clearly, Ofsted's school inspection findings confirm the importance and impact of the *Every Child Matters: Change for Children* initiative. The following list identifies some of the most important aspects of *Every Child Matters*:

- *Every Child Matters* provides a benchmark for ensuring that the well-being of all children is good to outstanding, irrespective of who they are or where they live.
- *Every Child Matters* enables services to be designed around the needs of the child or young person (personalised).

- *Every Child Matters* aims for earlier intervention and provision to prevent problems arising in the first place.
- *Every Child Matters* aims to make services easily accessible, and to be conveniently located for service users (children, young people and families).
- *Every Child Matters* enables teachers to focus on pupils' learning, while multi-agency practitioners target removing barriers to learning resulting from poor health, social and emotional problems, or abuse and neglect.
- *Every Child Matters* provides a framework of procedures and protocols for assessment, referral and tiered service provision for children.
- *Every Child Matters* reinforces the basic rights of every child and young person to be literate, numerate, healthy, safe from harm and to have a 'voice' and choice.

How to manage change for *Every Child Matters*

Change is a developmental process which aims to improve practice, introduce new policies and functions, promote working in a new way, and alter the 'status quo'. The process of change for *Every Child Matters* ideally needs to be culturally based, whereby schools/settings think collectively at a strategic and operational level about all five of the *ECM* well-being outcomes, and how these can be embedded into current practice.

As an individual practitioner and member of the children's workforce in a school or other educational setting, there are key stages in coping with and managing change for *Every Child Matters*. Tables 2.1 and 2.2 both illustrate the typical stages of change for *Every Child Matters*, and how to manage each.

Table 2.1 A staged approach to managing change for *Every Child Matters*

Stage of change for ECM	Strategies to manage change
A. The point at which the change for *ECM* is first announced. Reactions vary between excitement and anger.	Keep well-informed about planned change for *ECM* and the effect it might have on individuals. Be very clear about the reasons for the change.
B. Change for *ECM* occurs with immediate feelings of elation or depression according to how unexpected the change is. Positive and negative feelings occur.	Support is required to help the individual through conflicting and confusing mood swings.
C. Denial of the magnitude of change for *ECM* with self-doubt and depression occurring sometimes.	Seek an active, empathetic listener who will listen to any concerns or negative feelings.
D. Acceptance that the change for *ECM* is not going to go away and that it is here to stay.	Begin to think about strategies and suggestions for ways forward.
E. Practical stage where the individual tries and tests out different ways of adapting to the change for *ECM*.	Suggestions and advice are welcomed by others. There is support in looking at different options and testing out the likely consequences of each.

Source: Adapted from NCSL 2002/2003.

Table 2.2 Michael Fullan's model of change

Dimensions of change	Features of change
1. Moral purpose	Underpinned by values and vision with the understanding that the change will make a positive difference to the lives of staff, pupils, parents, governors and the community.
2. Understanding change	Developing the capacity to problem solve; encouraging others to buy into the change; building the capacity for change through collaborative team building; listening to concerns of those who may have some reservations about the change.
3. Relationship building	Developing emotional intelligence, i.e. develop emotional sensitivity; manage own emotions and understand others' feelings; being empathetic.
4. Knowledge creation and sharing	Defining the learning and well-being community; raising awareness, developing skills, creating and sharing new knowledge.
5. Coherence making	Some creativity is encouraged to prevent stagnation, but not too much, which could lead to initiative fatigue and overload.

Source: Fullan 2002.

How schools are implementing *Every Child Matters*

An examination of best practice for *Every Child Matters* existing in UK schools reveals the following approaches:

- Strengthening and expanding the senior leadership team, and investing heavily in middle management to lead aspects of *ECM* staff training.
- Introducing and integrating the *ECM* principles into the curriculum via Personal, Social and Health Education (PSHE) and Citizenship lessons, as well as into the social life of the school/ setting.
- Including *Every Child Matters* in the school's/setting's mission statement.

- Having a strong commitment to pupil voice and choice, personalised learning, raising pupils' self-esteem and creating a safe and positive learning environment.
- Having a designated member of the senior leadership team who is responsible for *Every Child Matters* overall, and who provides support and referral to specialist services/external agencies.
- Integrating *ECM* themes into other mainstream curriculum areas.
- Weaving *ECM* principles into the daily life of the school, for example assemblies.
- Providing a quiet place/space for pupils to use for reflection and peace.
- Having a clear and consistent behaviour policy and anti-bullying policy, which are both kept under review, and engage pupils in the process.
- Implementing Assessment for Learning (AfL) and for *ECM* well-being across the curriculum, ensuring pupils and parents understand the process, and that pupils are engaged in self-review and target setting.
- Introducing the Key Worker concept for pupils.
- Involving practitioners from external agencies/services in school activities, and in whole-school staff professional development for *Every Child Matters*.
- Having very effective ICT systems to support *ECM* planning and monitoring of pupil progress in well-being and learning.
- Undertaking regular surveys of opinion on *Every Child Matters* in school, among a range of stakeholders, for example, pupils, staff, parents/carers, governors and partners/practitioners from other agencies and organisations, working directly with pupils in the school/setting.
- Undertaking an annual evaluation of the five *ECM* outcomes to identify good practice, as well as aspects of *Every Child Matters* that require further improvement or development.

Questions for reflection

- How does your school's/setting's values and mission statement reflect the *ECM* aims?
- How are different stakeholders being engaged with and involved in the development and review of *Every Child Matters* in your school/setting?
- What strategies are being adopted in your school/setting to enable you and other practitioners/stakeholders to understand and manage change for *Every Child Matters*?
- What is the vision for *Every Child Matters* in your school/setting?
- What specific features of your school's/setting's *ECM* values and culture do external partners and the local community acknowledge as being good?
- What part have you played/can you play in helping to develop, strengthen and embed a strong culture for *Every Child Matters* in your school/setting?

3

Implementing *Every Child Matters* in the classroom

> **This chapter will cover:**
> - what *Every Child Matters* looks like in the classroom;
> - *Every Child Matters* and personalised learning;
> - *Every Child Matters* across the curriculum;
> - assessment for pupils' *ECM* well-being outcomes;
> - the effective deployment of teaching assistants to support pupils' *ECM* well-being outcomes.

What *Every Child Matters* looks like in the classroom

The following top ten features will be apparent in the *ECM*-friendly classroom:

1. The five *ECM* outcomes are displayed on the classroom wall and they are referred to regularly by staff and pupils, as part of everyday practice.
2. A Pupils' Charter is also displayed on the classroom wall which reflects the *ECM* outcomes.
3. Pupils understand what the five *ECM* outcomes mean in relation to their well-being, and can give examples.
4. Pupils' work and achievements are displayed and organised, according to the *ECM* outcomes, on the classroom walls.
5. Pupils' portfolios of work and achievements are organised according to the *ECM* outcomes.
6. The school council's class representative reports back from school council meetings on the *ECM* outcomes.

7. The class teacher at the beginning of lessons shares with pupils which *ECM* outcome(s) will be covered in the session.
8. Teacher planning shows links to the *ECM* outcomes.
9. Pupils have an individual and a whole-class target set for *ECM* outcomes, which are reviewed regularly.
10. The class takes responsibility for updating their *ECM* webpage on the school website.

Every Child Matters and personalised learning

One of the five *ECM* outcomes relates to every child and young person enjoying and achieving their learning and recreation, in order to fulfil their potential. Personalised learning is the approach being promoted by the government to enable this *ECM* outcome to be met.

Personalised learning is the process of tailoring learning to the needs, interests, aptitudes and aspirations of each individual, including removing barriers to learning, in order to enable children and young people to reach their optimum potential.

The personalised-learning approach helps to bring out the best in every child and young person. It builds on their strengths; it enables them to develop a love of learning and purposeful recreation; it helps them to grow in confidence and to develop their independence; and it makes them feel valued for the contributions they make. Figure 3.1 summarises the five aspects of personalised learning.

The features of effective personalised learning for supporting *ECM*

The following features of personalised learning have the greatest impact on raising attainment and expectations in enabling pupils to enjoy and achieve, according to Department for Education and Skills (DfES) research published in 2007:

- giving pupils a genuine 'voice' and choice;
- employing assessment for learning;
- utilising pupil self- and peer assessment;
- target setting;

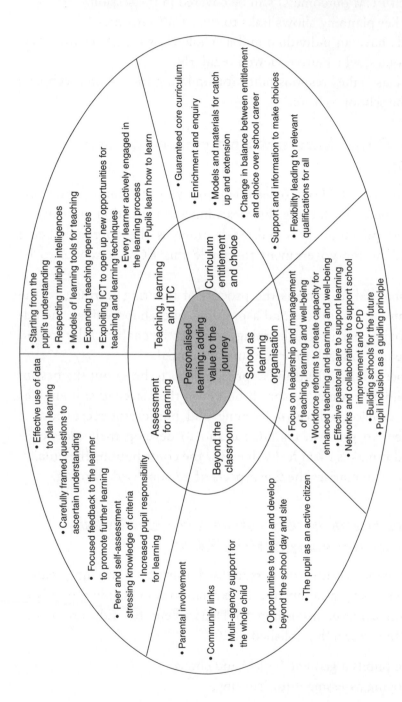

Figure 3.1 Aspects of personalised learning.

- tracking pupil progress;
- giving pupils greater responsibility for their own learning;
- mentoring and coaching pupils;
- drawing on pupils' prior experiences in lessons;
- high level of pupil participation in learning to learn;
- having a focus on utilising different learning styles and thinking skills;
- providing appropriate vocational and alternative flexible curriculum pathways;
- establishing strong links with the community to enhance learning and recreational opportunities;
- recognising the 'personal' element in teaching and supporting learning;
- effective deployment of teaching assistants, learning mentors and other practitioners delivering targeted interventions for underachieving pupils.

Every Child Matters across the curriculum

According to the Qualifications and Curriculum Authority (QCA) 2008, the five *ECM* outcomes need to be at the heart of everything a school does, and reinforced through every aspect of its curriculum. For example, in:

- *lessons* in different subjects;
- *events* such as sports days, drama productions, concerts and community activities;
- *routines* in school such as lunchtimes, assemblies, moving between lessons;
- the *environment* for learning, the culture or climate for learning and the physical aspects of the classrooms, school and its surroundings;
- *extended hours* offering opportunities to learners, families and communities before, during and after the school day, including links with social and health agencies;
- *out-of-school* learning – building on learning, knowledge, understanding and skills that pupils bring with them to school.

The new aims for the curriculum reflect the *ECM* outcomes. The curriculum should enable all children and young people to become:

- successful learners who enjoy learning, make progress and achieve;
- confident individuals who are able to lead safe, healthy and ful-filling lives;
- responsible citizens who make a positive contribution to society.

Table 3.1 (pp. 29–42) provides an overview of how each of the five *ECM* outcomes can be achieved in curriculum subjects. The QCA website provides further examples of how schools are building the five *ECM* outcomes into pupils' learning experiences (www.qca.org.uk/curriculum).

Assessment for *ECM* well-being outcomes

All those working directly with pupils in schools and other educational settings will need to assess pupils' *ECM* well-being outcomes (see Table 3.2, pp. 43–4). The principles of assessment for pupils' *ECM* well-being outcomes are similar to that of assessment for learning. As a process, assessment for *ECM* well-being gathers and interprets evidence for use by pupils and their teachers, to enable both to decide where pupils currently are in relation to their well-being outcomes, and to inform the next steps to achieve targets set for the five *ECM* outcomes. The key features of effective assessment for *ECM* well-being outcomes include assessment which:

- is part of teacher planning;
- focuses on how pupils can improve their *ECM* well-being out-comes;
- is central to everyday *ECM* classroom practice;
- is a key professional skill for those working with pupils in schools/settings;
- is sensitive and constructive in its approach;
- improves pupil motivation to achieve better *ECM* well-being outcomes;
- promotes greater commitment and a shared understanding of how to assess *ECM* well-being, linking it to national criteria, for example, National Service Framework (NSF), Ofsted;

- helps pupils to know how to improve their *ECM* well-being;
- helps to develop pupils' capacity for self-assessing their *ECM* well-being outcomes;
- recognises the full range of *ECM* well-being achievements of all pupils.

The effective deployment of teaching assistants supporting *ECM* well-being

The role of the teaching assistant has extended to incorporate supporting pupils' *ECM* well-being outcomes, as a result of the government's *ECM* strategy.

Effective collaborative partnership working between teachers and teaching assistants is crucial in order to ensure pupils reach their optimum potential in learning and well-being.

The following features are essential for teachers to ensure the effective deployment of teaching assistants (TAs) to support the *ECM* well-being outcomes:

- Ensure that teacher planning indicates clearly how TAs will be deployed for supporting the *ECM* outcomes.
- Clarify shared responsibilities for managing pupil behaviour and well-being.
- Make explicit the lesson objectives and expected pupil outcomes for *Every Child Matters*.
- Guide the teaching assistant in using effective support approaches and strategies that will enhance and improve pupils' *ECM* outcomes.
- Encourage the use of ICT and other multi-media technology to support improvement in pupils' *ECM* outcomes.
- Model good practice in relation to assessment for learning and *ECM* well-being to TAs, who can use this effectively with pupils.
- In partnership with TAs, tailor curriculum materials to incorporate the *ECM* outcomes.
- Capitalise on the strengths, expertise and talents of the TA in relation to developing and improving pupils' *ECM* well-being outcomes.

- Give the TA regular opportunities to feed back on the impact of their support and interventions in improving pupils' *ECM* well-being outcomes.
- Establish agreed procedures and ground rules for confidentiality and information sharing.
- Ensure a healthy and safe working environment is maintained.
- Ensure that the TA has the opportunity to contribute to the Common Assessment Framework (CAF) process, where appropriate, and that they are well-briefed before attending any pupil-review meetings.

Questions for reflection
- How are the *ECM* well-being outcomes linking to teaching and learning in your classroom?
- How do you ensure that you have good evidence of what you are doing for each of the five *ECM* outcomes?
- Which aspects of *Every Child Matters* are you finding it more difficult to cover in your classroom practice?
- How are you going to fill these gaps in *ECM* coverage?
- How are you involving pupils, teaching assistants and learning mentors in assessing pupil progress in the *ECM* well-being outcomes?
- How are you keeping track of all the pupils' interventions for *Every Child Matters*?
- How are these interventions informing your work in class?
- How effective has your work been with pupils in addressing the *ECM* outcomes in the classroom?

Table 3.1 The *Every Child Matters* outcomes across the curriculum

	Be healthy	Stay safe	Enjoy and achieve	Make a positive contribution	Achieve economic well-being
What pupils need to learn	• Importance of eating sensibly • Staying physically active and getting enough rest • How to make positive choices and take sensible actions • How to protect their emotional, social and mental well-being • The long-term consequences of the lifestyle choices they make now.	• How to identify and minimise risk • How to make informed safe choices • How to voice their opinions and resist unhelpful peer pressure.	• How to work imaginatively and creatively to develop new ideas, insights and ways of doing things • How to assess their skills, achievements and potential in order to set personal goals and achieve their best • The joy to be gained from successful learning.	• To form positive relationships and avoid bullying and discriminatory behaviour • About the different roles that people play in a community • How they can contribute to their own school and the wider community • How to work effectively with others.	• About the global economy and how businesses work • The qualities and skills needed for adult working life • To be enterprising • How to manage their own money.

Table 3.1 (*Continued*)

	Be healthy	Stay safe	Enjoy and achieve	Make a positive contribution	Achieve economic well-being
Art and design	• Exploring and expressing personal concerns and emotions.	• Following safe practices in the working environment • Forming and expressing opinions about art • Exploring identity and place in the world.	• Participating in creative, meaningful and intelligent making • Expressing themselves in new and original ways • Working in active learning environments.	• Collaborating with others on projects • Exploring the role of art, craft and design across times and cultures.	• Developing skills in critical thinking and creative problem solving • Learning about the creative industries • Working with artists and designers.

Table 3.1 (*Continued*)

Citizenship				
• Being empowered through taking action and making decisions • Learning about identity, diversity and respecting difference • Learning about the politics of everyday life.	• Asking questions rather than taking things at face value • Forming and expressing opinions • Making responsible decisions • Exploring controversial issues and situations • Examining the consequences of different actions • Learning how to seek help and advice • Reducing risk when working in the wider community.	• Participating in decision making • Working with others to campaign for change • Taking part in debates and finding out more about local and global issues • Using ICT or media such as film, drama and art to present and express ideas.	• Taking action on real issues and problems facing individuals and communities • Working with others to try to influence, change or resist unwanted change • Developing the knowledge, skills and confidence to participate effectively, responsibly and democratically • Lobbying or campaigning on issues.	• Finding creative solutions to problems • Expressing ideas and views effectively • Negotiating • Influencing others • Learning about economic dimensions of political and social decisions • Exploring the choices that governments have to make regarding taxation and public-spending priorities.

Table 3.1 (Continued)

	Be healthy	Stay safe	Enjoy and achieve	Make a positive contribution	Achieve economic well-being
Design and technology	• Understanding food hygiene • Learning about the relationship between food, health, growth and energy balance • Learning to prepare healthy food • Investigating products to protect health.	• Following safe practices in the workshop • Managing risk when using tools and equipment • Thinking about the safety of others.	• Creating practical products in response to people's needs or wants • Researching ideas and engaging with the world beyond school.	• Engaging in collaborative problem-solving activities • Designing products that contribute positively to the community or environment.	• Generating practical cost-effective solutions that are relevant and fit for purpose • Solving technical problems • Responding creatively to briefs • Developing proposals • Working with designers • Exploring career opportunities in design.

Table 3.1 (*Continued*)

English				
• Reading and writing for pleasure • Exploring issues and expressing feelings through prose, poetry, drama and role play • Reading to access health information.	• Developing the confidence to ask questions and express opinions • Assessing the validity of opinions and information • Exploring situations, dilemmas and relationships through texts, role play and drama.	• Experiencing the richness and breadth of literature • Expressing ideas and opinions • Creating new worlds in poetry and narrative • Developing confidence through drama.	• Working collaboratively as part of a group discussion or drama activities • Providing constructive responses to others' work • Speaking, listening and writing for purposes beyond the classroom • Contributing to school life through drama.	• Developing communication skills and literacy • Expressing ideas and views effectively • Exploring career opportunities in the creative and cultural industries.

Table 3.1 (*Continued*)

	Be healthy	Stay safe	Enjoy and achieve	Make a positive contribution	Achieve economic well-being
Geography	• Investigating illness and disease around the world • Comparing lifestyles in different countries.	• Developing safe working practices while carrying out fieldwork • Exploring hazards and health risks in areas where people are not safe • Questioning information and opinions and not taking things at face value.	• Learning about different environments, places, cultures and peoples • Taking part in fieldwork • Developing a sense of curiosity about the Earth.	• Considering their role as world citizens • Learning about sustainable development • Examining the social, environmental and economic impacts of what people do individually and collectively.	• Exploring how nations and peoples trade • Researching, presenting and analysing information • Appreciating the need for sustainable economic developments.

Table 3.1 *(Continued)*

History					
• Learning about personal and public health and their impact on life • Exploring individual identity through personal and community history.	• Developing safe working practices while carrying out fieldwork and other investigations • Exploring events in the past when people have not been safe • Challenging information and being aware of bias and inaccuracies.	• Discovering rich and varied stories from the past • Taking part in investigations and fieldwork • Visiting museums, galleries and historical sites • Connecting life today to life in the past.	• Learning about the lives of famous philanthropists • Researching local history to find out who has helped to improve the community and how • Learning how populations have pulled together in times of war.	• Exploring how working patterns and the nature of work have changed over time • Challenging information and being aware of bias and inaccuracies • Expressing ideas and views effectively • Engaging in critical research.

Table 3.1 (*Continued*)

	Be healthy	Stay safe	Enjoy and achieve	Make a positive contribution	Achieve economic well-being
ICT	• Accessing information on health and well-being • Analysing nutritional data using monitoring technology during exercise.	• Developing safe practice when using ICT (e.g. correct positioning of equipment and chairs, taking regular breaks) • Questioning information and not accepting it at face value • Learning responsible use of email and the internet • Avoiding disclosure of personal details.	• Using ICT to support creativity, initiative and independent thinking • Conveying ideas in original ways • Using ICT to work collaboratively • Using ICT for music, film and photography.	• Accessing information and ideas on local, national and international issues • Sharing information with people from diverse backgrounds • Learning about equality of access, copyright and plagiarism • Using forums.	• Learning when and how to use ICT skills to support work • Developing ICT capability • Obtaining, analysing and presenting information • Using ICT to collaborate with others • Learning how to manage finances online.

Table 3.1 (*Continued*)

Mathematics	• Investigating numerical data related to health and diet • Becoming financially capable and gaining greater control over factors affecting health.	• Understanding risk through the study of probability • Making informed choices about investments, loans and gambling.	• Developing mathematical ways of perceiving the world • Recognising underlying structures and connections between mathematical ideas • Investigating games and strategies.	• Learning to use logic, data and generalisations with precision.	• Understanding and managing money • Making sound economic decisions in daily life • Learning about investments • Reasoning with numbers • Interpreting graphs and diagrams • Communicating maths information.
Modern foreign language	• Building confidence through speaking another language • Gaining new perspective on the world and life in other countries.	• Communicating with strangers • Dealing with unfamiliar situations in which communication is difficult • Understanding others' customs and avoiding difficult or dangerous situations in travel.	• Extending horizons beyond this country • Learning to communicate with people from different parts of the world • Learning about different cultures and countries • Gaining a sense of achievement from successful communication.	• Actively trying to understand and communicate with others • Learning to be 'ambassadors' for their own country and culture.	• Learning to use business-related language • Preparing to work in the international market.

Table 3.1 *(Continued)*

	Be healthy	Stay safe	Enjoy and achieve	Make a positive contribution	Achieve economic well-being
Music	• Improving physical, mental and emotional well-being through singing, playing and listening to music.	• Developing critical skills and self-discipline • Forming and expressing opinions about music.	• Gaining enjoyment from performing, composing and listening • Taking part in musical activities and events • Playing music with others.	• Contributing to school life as a performer, listener, organiser, music leader or in a supporting role.	• Working as part of a team to play or compose music • Learning about the music industry.

Table 3.1 (*Continued*)

PE				
• Taking part in high-quality physical activity • Developing a fitness programme • Seeing physical activity as part of a lifelong healthy lifestyle • Expressing emotions through dance • Enjoying watching sport • Learning about how the body works and why exercise and rest are important • Exploring dietary habits.	• Learning the importance of following rules • Taking part safely in outdoor and adventurous activities • Minimising risk in physical activity.	• Participating and achieving as performers, officials and leaders • Making links with physical activities, sport and dance in the community • Taking part in creative, artistic, aesthetic, competitive and challenging activities • Working as part of a team.	• Contributing to school life through sport • Helping as an official, coach or administrator • Contributing to a team performance • Developing an understanding of fairness • Working collaboratively on problem-solving challenges.	• Working individually and as part of a team • Reviewing, refining and carrying out plans • Learning about balancing work with leisure and social interaction • Exploring career opportunities in sport.

Table 3.1 *(Continued)*

	Be healthy	Stay safe	Enjoy and achieve	Make a positive contribution	Achieve economic well-being
PSHE	• Learning about diet and healthy living • Developing drug awareness • Learning about sexual health • Exploring self-identity and image • Managing risk and dealing with social and moral dilemmas • Withstanding peer pressure.	• Managing risk • Developing safe working practices while engaged in work experience and enterprise activities • Exploring personal, ethical and moral issues • Developing first-aid skills • Forming safe relationships • Avoiding debt and financial hardship.	• Learning practical, real-life skills • Taking part in enterprise activities • Meeting new people.	• Working collaboratively on group activities getting involved with the local community.	• Learning about progression routes into further education, employment and training • Finding creative solutions to problems • Learning to be adaptable • Expressing ideas and views effectively • Working well in groups • Engaging in critical research • Evaluating evidence • Identifying and analysing different interpretations of issues and events • Substantiating arguments and judgements.

RE					
	• Exploring morals and decision making • Learning about sexual health and ethics • Exploring mediation and enlightenment • Learning about spiritual rituals.	• Evaluating ideas, relationships and practices • Learning about religious and ethical rules governing care of children, respect for friends and neighbours and responsibility for crime • Learning about authority ethics, relationships and rights and responsibilities.	• Exploring and sharing beliefs, practices and feelings • Engaging with issues of meaning and value • Developing curiosity about religion in the modern world • Searching for meaning • Debating ideas, meeting people of different cultures and beliefs.	• Developing an appreciation of different points of view • Investigating, discussing and building reasoned arguments • Dealing with different beliefs respectfully • Learning about justice, authority and interfaith dialogue • Learning about faith groups in the community.	• Learning about religious and ethical rules surrounding the use of money • Learning about equality, justice, prejudice, discrimination, human rights, fair trade, the environment and climate change • Learning about religious issues in the workplace, such as diet, clothing, use of time for prayer, values and attitudes • Learning about the work of charities • Developing skills of listening, empathy and group collaboration.

Table 3.1 *(Continued)*

	Be healthy	Stay safe	Enjoy and achieve	Make a positive contribution	Achieve economic well-being
Science	• Learning about diets, drugs, disease and contraception • Understanding the consequences of poor diet and the misuse of alcohol and drugs.	• Following safe working practices in a laboratory • Assessing and managing risk through scientific experiments • Handling chemicals and biological materials safely • Using electricity, heat and light safely.	• Developing curiosity about the world • Carrying out practical investigations • Exploring the effect of science on lives on a personal, local, national and global scale.	• Actively contributing to scientific investigations • Learning about the relationship between science, society and the future of the world • Considering ethical and moral issues • Learning about global sustainability.	• Obtaining, analysing, evaluating and communicating data • Engaging in critical research • Exploring career opportunities in science.

Source: QCA 2008.

Table 3.2 Assessment for *Every Child Matters* well-being outcomes

Be healthy	Stay safe	Enjoy and achieve	Make a positive contribution	Achieve economic well-being
Assessment descriptors	Assessment descriptors	Assessment descriptors	Assessment descriptors	Assessment descriptors
I have eaten healthy meals at lunchtimes	I always consider the safety of others	My achievements are valued in school	My views and opinions have been listened to in school	I have participated in mini-enterprise activities in school
I have drunk water throughout the day	I have reported a bullying incident to a member of staff in school	I only miss school when I am ill	I complete an annual pupil survey which seeks my views	I have worked as a member of a team to solve problems
I have undertaken PE, sports and games each week	I always take note of warning signs about hazards or dangers	I am involved in setting targets for my learning and well-being	I follow the principles on the Pupils' Charter	I know the importance of being able to manage my own money/savings
I have disposed of litter correctly, and kept my learning environment clean and tidy	I have played safely at break and lunchtimes due to staff being on duty	I regularly review my own progress and discuss this with teachers and staff supporting me	I have raised issues with the class School Council Rep. when I think there is a need to do so	I know what local businesses there are in the community
I have made use of the outdoor play space	I have followed safety rules in the classroom and around school	I have contributed to classroom displays of pupils' work and achievements	I have contributed to fund-raising and volunteering	I have been given advice on future learning and career pathways
There is an adult/key worker who I trust and can go to when troubled or worried	I am aware of community safety issues, i.e. stranger danger, road safety	I enjoy practical work and working with others	I have posted my thoughts and questions in the suggestion box in class	I have had the opportunity to attend study support and challenge sessions

Table 3.2 *(Continued)*

Be healthy	Stay safe	Enjoy and achieve	Make a positive contribution	Achieve economic well-being
Calm music helps me to relax	I have followed safety rules when out on school trips, school residentials, fieldwork	I have used different learning styles in lessons	I have voted on important school issues when requested to do so	I have had a position of responsibility in class this year
The quiet area/peace zone is accessed in school when I need it	I always use equipment, chemicals and medicines correctly, and store these in a safe place under adult supervision	I have used ICT and other multi-media technology to support my learning and well-being	I understand and know the rights that children have (UNCRC)	I have had good advice on how to cope with any change in school or out of school at home from the support staff
I always respect the feelings and views of others	I ensure that I do not block access routes for the disabled	I have participated in after-school and lunchtime activities	I have participated in a pupil buddying/mentoring scheme	I have some knowledge of the benefits and services available in the community
I have accessed further information about healthy eating and lifestyles	I ensure that outdoor areas I access at school are secure and well lit	I have enjoyed working with artists in residence, sports coaches and external experts	I know my confidence has increased because of staff support	I have had the opportunity to take initiative in class this year

Notes:
- Pupils can self-assess their *ECM* outcome achievements by highlighting the outcomes descriptors achieved above.
- Staff can cross-check the pupils' self-assessment by highlighting outcomes achieved in a different colour.

4

Monitoring and evaluating the *Every Child Matters* outcomes

This chapter will cover:

- clarification of the terms *monitoring* and *evaluation*;
- how to collect *ECM* data and track ongoing pupil progress in relation to monitoring the *ECM* outcomes;
- gathering evidence on the *ECM* outcomes for the Ofsted school self-evaluation form (SEF);
- how to involve key stakeholders (pupils, parents/carers and practitioners) in evaluating the impact of any additional provision or interventions on improving the *ECM* outcomes.

Monitoring and evaluation: understanding the terminology

Monitoring is the process of checking progress against set targets in relation to the *ECM* outcomes. It also looks at trends in *ECM* performance indicators. Monitoring is also concerned with the systematic, regular gathering of information about the extent to which agreed or required plans, policies or statutory requirements for *Every Child Matters* are being implemented. *Evaluation* describes the activity of critically examining and judging the quality and effectiveness of provision for *Every Child Matters* and the impact on pupils' outcomes, based on evidence collected by the review and monitoring process. Evaluation is also concerned with gauging effectiveness, strengths and weaknesses, and interpreting how well activities, interventions and initiatives for *Every Child Matters* are progressing.

Collecting *ECM* outcomes data to track pupil progress

Data for *ECM* outcomes will be quantitative and qualitative. The qualitative data are likely to be subjective to some extent, because it is about 'soft' outcomes and human relationships, which may not always be measurable or quantifiable, for example, self-esteem and self-confidence. Quantitative data for *Every Child Matters* will be related to 'hard' evidence such as: school attendance; number of exclusions; frequency of use and take up of extended services; impact measures as a result of additional interventions; or the number of school-level indicators for *ECM* well-being outcomes that pupils achieve.

This section of the chapter offers a couple of practical examples to all those front-line practitioners working directly with children and young people in schools and other educational settings, for tracking pupil-level progress towards meeting the *ECM* well-being outcomes.

Tables 4.1 and 4.2 and Figure 4.1 can be adapted and modified to suit the school's/setting's own monitoring systems. However, they do offer a starting point for having a greater focus on tracking *ECM* well-being outcomes at pupil level, to the same extent as tracking pupil progress in relation to academic attainment. The *ECM* outcomes tracking grid featured in Table 4.1 requires the practitioner to record the names of the pupils at each termly interval, in relation to each aspect of the five *ECM* well-being outcomes. This enables those monitoring pupils' well-being progress to find the answers to the following questions:

- Are pupils making good enough progress throughout the school year?
- Are any pupils 'stuck', and not making good progress in *Every Child Matters*?
- If pupils are stuck at an aspect of an *ECM* outcome, how does the practitioner, along with others, intend to improve progress?
- Overall, which *ECM* outcomes do pupils make the most progress in?
- Overall, which *ECM* outcomes do pupils make the least progress in and why?
- What action will you take, along with other practitioners, to ensure improvement occurs in the poorer aspects of *ECM* outcomes?

Table 4.1 Tracking grid to monitor pupils' progress in *Every Child Matters* well-being outcomes

	Every Child Matters aims	*Autumn term*	*Spring term*	*Summer term*
Be healthy	1.1 Physically healthy: regular exercise; five hours of PE a week			
	1.2 Mentally and emotionally healthy: recognise the signs of personal stress and develop strategies to manage it			
	1.3 Sexually healthy: understand sexual health risks			
	1.4 Live healthy lifestyles: make informed healthy lifestyle choices; eat and drink healthily			
	1.5 Choose not to take illegal drugs: understand the dangers of smoking and substance abuse			
Stay safe	2.1 Safe from maltreatment, neglect, violence and sexual exploitation			
	2.2 Safe from accidental injury and death: act responsibly in high-risk situations; physical activities undertaken in an orderly and sensible manner			
	2.3 Safe from bullying and discrimination: also feel confident to report bullying and racist incidents			
	2.4 Safe from crime and anti-social behaviour in and out of school: refrain from intimidating and anti-social behaviour; display concern for others			
	2.5 Have security, stability and be cared for			

From: Cheminais, Rita, *The Pocket Guide to Every Child Matters*, London: Routledge, © Rita Cheminais 2010.

Table **4.1** *(Continued)*

	Every Child Matters aims	Autumn term	Spring term	Summer term
Enjoy and achieve	3.1 Ready for school: have positive attitudes to education			
	3.2 Attend and enjoy school: have a good school attendance record; enjoy their learning very much			
	3.3 Achieve stretching national educational standards in primary school: make good progress in their learning			
	3.4 Achieve personal and social development and enjoy recreation: good personal development evidenced by high self-esteem; have high aspirations and increasing independence; behave well			
	3.5 Achieve stretching national educational standards in secondary school: make good progress in their learning			
Make a positive contribution	4.1 Engage in decision making and support the community and environment: involved in school and community activities; able to express their views at school and are confident their views and 'voice' will be heard			
	4.2 Engage in law-abiding and positive behaviour in and out of school: understand their legal and civil rights and responsibilities; show social responsibility			
	4.3 Develop positive relationships and choose not to bully or discriminate			
	4.4 Develop self-confidence and successfully deal with significant life changes and challenges			
	4.5 Develop enterprising behaviour			

From: Cheminais, Rita, *The Pocket Guide to Every Child Matters*, London: Routledge, © Rita Cheminais 2010.

Table 4.1 (*Continued*)

Achieve economic well-being	5.1 Engage in further education, employment or training on leaving school: become enterprising and able to handle change in their lives				
	5.2 Ready for employment: develop knowledge and skills for when they are older, related to workplace situations; develop basic skills in literacy, numeracy and ICT; develop their self-confidence and team working skills; take initiative and calculate risk when making decisions; become financially literate and gain an understanding of business and the economy, and of their career options				
	5.3 Live in decent homes and sustainable communities				
	5.4 Have access to transport and material goods				
	5.5 Live in households free from low income				

Notes:

How to use the *ECM* outcomes tracking grid:

- Put the initials or names of each pupil in your class/group who achieves any *ECM* outcome aims for each term, as they progress through the school year.
- When you have tracked pupils for the school year on the grid above, identify any pupils who have gaps in their *ECM* outcomes.
- From your annual monitoring of pupils' *ECM* outcomes, which aspects do you need to target further, and how?

From: Cheminais, Rita, *The Pocket Guide to Every Child Matters*, London: Routledge, © Rita Cheminais 2010.

Table 4.2 Tracking sheet for individual pupils', a group of pupils' or a class's *Every Child Matters* well-being outcomes

TERM & YEAR: _____ PRACTITIONER: _____

Unique Pupil Number (UPN) and/or pupil name	D.O.B.	Ethnicity	Attendance	Behaviour/ exclusions	Be healthy	Stay safe	Enjoy and achieve	Positive contribution	Achieve economic well-being

Key to scores (Based on the Ofsted grades: 1 = outstanding; 2 = good; 3 = satisfactory; 4 = inadequate). Using the Ofsted judgement criteria, place an appropriate score for each pupil you support, related to the five *Every Child Matters* well-being outcomes.

From: Cheminais, Rita, *The Pocket Guide to Every Child Matters*, London: Routledge, © Rita Cheminais 2010.

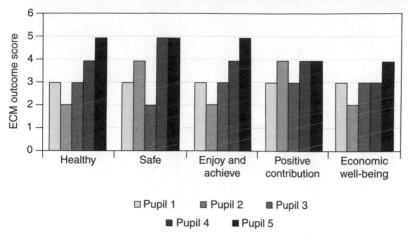

Figure 4.1 Recording pupils' overall *Every Child Matters* outcomes.

Table 4.2 utilises the Ofsted judgement grading scores of 1 to 4:

1 = outstanding; 2 = good; 3 = satisfactory; 4 = inadequate

Figure 4.1 utilises the following point-score scale for recording pupils' progress in each of the five *ECM* outcomes' aims: 0 = no evidence; 1 = one *ECM* outcome aim met; 2 = two *ECM* outcome aims met; 3 = three *ECM* outcome aims met; 4 = four *ECM* outcome aims met; 5 = five *ECM* outcome aims fully met.

Gathering evidence on the *ECM* outcomes for the Ofsted self-evaluation form

Gathering evidence on the *ECM* outcomes from the impact of teaching, support and targeted interventions on improving pupils' well-being is an ongoing process. Table 4.3 provides a list of evidence with performance indicators, where relevant, which will enable class teachers and others working directly with pupils to know what the expectations are in terms of evidence to be gathered and the criteria for judging the impact. Table 4.4 summarises the National Service Framework Standards, referred to in Table 4.3. Class teachers, TAs, learning mentors and other practitioners from the children's workforce will need to take note of the school-level indicators for pupil well-being which the Department for Children, Schools and Families (DCSF) and Ofsted have produced.

Table 4.3 Gathering evidence on *Every Child Matters* outcomes for the self-evaluation form

Every Child Matters outcomes	*Evidence and impact*
Be healthy • Pupils show a good understanding of how they can live a healthy lifestyle. • Pupils know how to maintain good physical health. • Pupils have developed good emotional health and well-being. • Pupils understand the risks to their sexual health. • Pupils are aware of the dangers of smoking and drug/substance abuse to their health. • Pupils are consulted on and involved in any decision making related to their health.	**Performance indicators** • % increase of pupils having a healthy breakfast to start their day • % increase of pupils participating in regular exercise • % increase of pupils feeling that they are able to access appropriate support if they feel troubled or worried • NSF Standard 1 met • NSF Standard 9 met
Stay safe • Pupils feel safe from bullying, discrimination and racism. • Pupils have regard to the dignity, safety and well-being of others. • Pupils do not behave anti-socially. • Pupils know their views are listened to and are confident with the adult support provided. • Pupils act responsibly and are able to assess risk. • Pupils are protected from danger in school. • Pupils are receptive to the support and help given to them by other agencies. • Pupils respect the wishes of others.	**Performance indicators** • % decrease in the number of pupils being subjected to bullying • % decrease in the number of pupils being re-registered on the Child Protection register • Record of positive action taken for all child protection referrals • NSF Standard 2 met • NSF Standard 5 met

Table 4.3 *(Continued)*

	Performance indicators
Enjoy and achieve • Pupils make good progress in relation to their starting points. • Pupils achieve their optimum potential. • Pupils' needs are catered for through personalised curriculum pathways. • Pupils are active participants in their own learning and in aspects of school life. • Pupils' achievements are valued. • Pupils have positive attitudes to learning. • Pupils enjoy learning and attending school.	• % increase of pupils attending school • % increase of pupils reporting that they enjoy school • % increase of pupils making progress in their learning and well-being • % increase of pupils participating in recreational lunchtime and after-school activities • NSF Standard 9 met
Make a positive contribution • Pupils are able to form stable relationships with others. • Pupils are able to manage change in their own lives. • Pupils can express their views and participate in decision making in relation to school matters and their own lives. • Pupils show good commitment to supporting others in school and in the community. • Pupils subscribe to the school's view about what makes a worthwhile positive contribution. • Pupils engage with volunteering activities. • Pupils understand how to become a responsible citizen.	• % increase of pupils participating in community and voluntary activities • % increase of pupils making positive progress following transfer and transition between key stages • % increase of pupils participating in decision making activities within school

Table 4.3 (*Continued*)

Every Child Matters outcomes	*Evidence and impact*
Achieve economic well-being • Pupils are able to work independently and cooperatively. • Pupils have acquired the basic skills in literacy, numeracy and ICT. • Pupils have developed financial literacy. • Pupils have a knowledge about enterprise and participate in enterprising activities such as fundraising for charity. • Pupils have the skills to prepare them for later life – work and adulthood. • Pupils have clear career pathways, and engage in FE, training or employment on leaving school.	**Performance indicators** • % increase of pupils going on to HE, FE or into employment • % increase of disaffected/disengaged pupils participating in targeted learning programmes • In-depth evaluation showing the impact of specific intervention programmes, e.g. work-related learning, work placements, college link courses

Table 4.4 National Service Framework Standards for children, young people and maternity services

Standard title	Standard descriptor	Main themes in Standard
1. Promoting health and well-being, identifying needs and intervening early	The health and well-being of all children and young people is promoted and delivered through a coordinated programme of action, including prevention and early intervention wherever possible, to ensure long-term gain led by the NHS in partnership with local authorities.	• Child Health Programme to reduce health inequalities. • Multi-agency health promotion. • Healthy lifestyles promoted. • Universal and targeted health promotion. • Access to targeted services. • Early intervention and assessing needs.
2. Supporting parenting	Parents and carers are enabled to receive the information, services and support which will help them to care for their children and equip them with the skills they need to ensure that their children have optimum life chances and are healthy and safe.	• Universal, targeted and specialist services to support mothers and fathers. • Up-to-date information and education for parents. • Support for parents of pre-school children to help children develop secure attachments and to develop. • Support for parents of school-aged children to involve them in their child's learning and behaviour management. • Early, multi-agency support for parents with specific needs, i.e. mental health problems, addiction to drugs, alcohol; parents of disabled children, teenage parents. • Coordinated services across child and adult services. • Multi-disciplinary support to meet the needs of adoptive parents/adults caring for looked-after children.

Table 4.4 (Continued)

Standard title	Standard descriptor	Main themes in Standard
3. Child, young person and family-centred services	Children and young people and families receive high-quality services which are coordinated around their individual and family needs and take account of their views.	• Appropriate information to children, young people and their parents. • Listening and responding to them in relation to their care and treatment. • Services respectful of the wishes of children and young people. • Improved access to services. • Robust multi-agency planning and commissioning arrangements, i.e. Children's Trusts, Common Assessment Framework. • Quality and safety of care in delivery of child-centred services. • Common core of skills, knowledge and competences for staff working with children and young people, across all agencies.

Table 4.4 (*Continued*)

4. Growing up into adulthood	All young people have access to age-appropriate services which are responsive to their specific needs as they grow into adulthood.	• Confidentiality and consent for young people. • Health promotion to meet needs, i.e. reduce teenage pregnancy, smoking, substance misuse, suicide, sexually transmitted infections. • Support achievement of full potential, e.g. Connexions and Youth Services. • Improved access to services and advice for those who are disabled, in special circumstances or who live in rural areas. • Transition to full adult services. • Additional support available for looked-after children leaving care and other young people in special circumstances.
5. Safeguarding and promoting the welfare of children and young people	All agencies work to prevent children suffering harm and to promote their welfare, provide them with the services they require to address their identified needs and safeguard children who are being or who are likely to be harmed.	• All agencies prioritise safeguarding and promoting the welfare of children. • LA children and Young People's Plan. • Clarification of agencies' roles and responsibilities. • Profile of local population to identify and assess vulnerable children. • High-quality integrated services to meet needs of children at risk of harm, abuse or neglect. • Effective supervision for staff working with children to ensure clear, accurate, comprehensive, up-to-date records are kept, and high-quality services delivered.

Table 4.4 (*Continued*)

Standard title	Standard descriptor	Main themes in Standard
6. Children and young people who are ill	All children and young people who are ill or thought to be ill or injured will have timely access to appropriate advice and to effective services which address their health, social, educational and emotional needs throughout the period of their illness.	• Comprehensive, integrated, timely local services. • Professionals support children, young people and their families in self-care of their illness. • Access to advice and services in a range of settings. • Trained, competent professionals providing consistent advice to assist and treat a child who is ill. • High-quality treatment, and high-quality care for those with long-term conditions. • Prevention, assessment and treatment of pain management improved. • Integrated Children's Community teams and Community Children's nursing services working outside hospital.
7. Children and young people in hospital	Children and young people receive high-quality, evidence-based hospital care, developed through clinical governance and delivered in appropriate settings.	• Care integrated and coordinated around their needs. Play for children in hospital is essential. • Children, young people and their families treated with respect, involved in decision making about their care, and given choices. • Planned discharge from hospital for children. • Hospital stay kept to a minimum. • High-quality evidence-based care provided. • Hospitals meet responsibilities to safeguard and promote welfare of children. • Care is provided in an appropriate location and in a safe environment.

Table 4.4 (*Continued*)

8. **Disabled children and young people and those with complex health needs**	Children and young people who are disabled or who have complex health needs, receive coordinated, high-quality child- and family-centred services which are based on assessed needs, which promote social inclusion and, where possible, enable them and their families to live ordinary lives.	• Services promote social inclusion. • Increased access to hospital and primary health-care services, therapy and equipment services, and social services. • Early identification of health conditions, impairments and physical barriers to inclusion through integrated diagnosis and assessment processes. • Early intervention and support for parents. • Palliative care is available where needed. • Services have robust systems to safeguard disabled children and young people. • Multi-agency transition planning occurs to support adulthood.
9. **The mental health and psychological well-being of children and young people**	All children and young people, from birth to their eighteenth birthday, who have mental health problems and disorders have access to timely, integrated, high-quality multi-disciplinary mental health services to ensure effective assessment, treatment and support, for them and their families.	• Professional support for children's mental health is available in the early years. • Staff working with children and young people contribute to early intervention and mental health promotion and develop good partnerships with children. • Improved access to CAMHS with high-quality multi-disciplinary CAMHS teams working in a range of settings. • Gaps in service addressed particularly for those with learning disabilities. • Care Networks developed and care in appropriate and safe settings.

Table 4.4 *(Continued)*

Standard title	Standard descriptor	Main themes in Standard
10. Medicines for children and young people	Children, young people, their parents or carers, and health-care professionals in all settings make decisions about medicines based on sound information about risk and benefit. They have access to safe and effective medicines that are prescribed on the basis of the best available evidence.	• Safe medication practice. • Use of unlicensed and off-label medicines comply with local and safety standards. • Enhanced decision support for prescribers. • Improved access to medicines. • Clear, understandable, up-to-date information provided on medicines to users and parents. • Greater support for those taking medication at home, in care and in education settings – safe storage, supply and administration of medicines. • Equitable access to medicines and to safeguard children in special circumstances, disabled children and those with mental health disorders. • Pharmacists' expertise is fully utilised.
11. Maternity services	Women have easy access to supportive, high-quality maternity services, designed around their individual needs and those of their babies.	• Women-centred care with easy access to information and support. • Care pathways and managed care networks. • Improved pre-conception care and access to a midwife as first point of contact. • Local perinatal psychiatric services available. • Choice of where best to give birth, i.e. home or maternity unit. • Post-birth care provided based on a structured assessment. • Breast-feeding information and support for mothers.

Source: DFES/DH 2004c.

School-level indicators for pupil well-being

Ofsted and the DCSF jointly have produced a set of standardised school-level indicators for evaluating pupil well-being, which apply to all maintained primary, secondary and special schools, Pupil Referral Units (PRUs) and academies. Two types of indicators are used for the school-level indicators:

1. *quantitative indicators* that the school has significant influence over, for example:
   - the school's overall attendance rate for the most recent school year;
   - the percentage of persistent absences;
   - the percentage of pupils doing at least two hours a week of high-quality PE and sport;
   - the take up of school lunches;
   - the rate of permanent exclusions;
   - (for secondary schools) post-16 progression measures, such as participation in learning in the year after they leave compulsory schooling.
2. *qualitative indicators* based on the perceptions of pupils and their parents/carers relating to the *ECM* outcomes. These indicators are derived from surveys of pupils' and parents'/carers' perceptions and will cover the extent to which the school:
   - promotes healthy eating;
   - promotes exercise and a healthy lifestyle and (for younger children) play;
   - discourages smoking, consumption of alcohol and the use of illegal drugs and other harmful substances;
   - gives good guidance on relationships and sexual health;
   - helps pupils to manage their feelings and be resilient;
   - promotes equality and counteracts discrimination;
   - provides a good range of educational activities;
   - gives pupils good opportunities to contribute to the local community;
   - helps people of different backgrounds to get on well, both in school and in the wider community;
   - helps pupils gain the knowledge and skills they will need in the future;

- offers the opportunity at 14 to access a range of curriculum choices;
- supports pupils to make choices that will help them progress towards a chosen career/subject of further study.

Qualitative indicators also cover the extent to which pupils:

- feel safe
- experience bullying
- know who to approach if they have a concern
- enjoy school
- are making good progress
- feel listened to
- are able to influence decisions in the school.

                                        (Source: Ofsted 2008d: 13)

The school-level indicators will help schools and other education settings to analyse and assess how well they are promoting the well-being of pupils, the strengths, weaknesses and impact of the school's contribution to improving pupils' well-being in partnership with others, and where the school/setting could improve its contribution to the *ECM* outcomes for its pupils. Schools supplement the indicators with their own data and qualitative evidence when self-evaluating and reviewing the impact of provision on pupils' well-being outcomes. Ofsted inspectors will look at the school's analysis of the indicators in its SEF. The School Profile will also include the school-level indicators for pupil well-being.

The revised inspection schedule for schools from September 2009 will have a stronger focus on the well-being of pupils. Ofsted inspectors will use the evidence from the school-level indicators to consider how effectively pupils' well-being is being promoted in the school. Inspectors want to know what the school's contribution to the well-being of pupils has been, if pupils' and parents'/carers' views on the *ECM* outcomes are being valued and what impact partnership arrangements and activities are having on pupils' well-being outcomes.

The DCSF guidance on the school's role in promoting pupil well-being gives examples of pupil well-being in practice, which cover the aspects that the school-level indicators focus on.

Table 4.5 Examples of pupil well-being in practice

Be healthy	Stay safe	Enjoy and achieve	Make a positive contribution	Achieve economic well-being
• Effective health education is delivered through well-planned PSHE, with inputs from health and other professionals. • Health service provision is on site. • Pupils know what support and services are available to them and how to access them.	• Signs of abuse or neglect are identified and concerns are referred to safeguarding services early. • The standards and advice on helping to ensure children are safe in the early years are followed. • Safe recruitment principles are used for staff – CRB checks. • There is good order and discipline, high standards of behaviour, and mutual respect to enable pupils to feel safe and know how to keep themselves safe.	• Effective personalised learning, one-to-one interventions, and taking effective action to narrow gaps in attainment and help pupils to catch up. • Curriculum and teaching is culturally sensitive, lively and engaging, tailored to pupils' interests and needs, stretching the most able to achieve their best. • A wide range of curriculum pathways at KS4 that suit different learning styles and abilities are offered.	• Sport, cultural and volunteering activities within and outside the regular school day are offered. • There is high-quality citizenship and RE delivered to help pupils understand how society works, to prepare them for playing their part as adult citizens and to help them understand other faiths and cultures while developing a sense of shared identity. • Opportunities are provided for pupils to interact, learn and work together with peers from different backgrounds.	• Pupils' personal, learning and thinking skills are developed, i.e. the ability to communicate clearly, resilience, initiative, enterprise, creativity and social and team-working skills. • Pupils have high-quality work experience and tasters of the world of work.

Table 4.5 *(Continued)*

Be healthy	Stay safe	Enjoy and achieve	Make a positive contribution	Achieve economic well-being
• The school environment promotes good physical health, including healthy weight, e.g. healthy, appetising school meals, healthy packed lunches; offers physical activities such as sports, dance, outdoor play, walking to school. • There is a supportive ethos where staff model positive behaviour, promote pupils' social, emotional and good positive mental health development, including pupils self-respect, and their respect for others through the SEAL programme.	• Complaints about bullying are dealt with swiftly, and any particular groups of pupils suffering disproportionate bullying are monitored. • Pupil absence is managed proactively, following up on pupils who are persistent absentees (missing 20% or more of school sessions), engaging with the child and their parents to improve attendance, and investigate and assess risk.	• All pupils have access to the full range of educational options, including the 14–19 Diplomas. • There is early intervention when pupils present social and behavioural problems, providing timely additional support on a multi-agency basis where appropriate to help pupils get back on track and reduce the need for a permanent exclusion.	• A rights-respecting culture exists which is demonstrated throughout the school; pupil voice and participation is encouraged in school decision making, and pupils are encouraged to respect responsibilities to each other.	• Young people have good quality, impartial advice and guidance at the right time that helps to raise aspirations about course options and career choices, working in partnership with other schools/colleges and Information Advice and Guidance providers. • The financial capability of pupils is improved to help them understand and prepare for the financial challenges of adult life.

Table 4.5 (*Continued*)

	• 'At risk' pupils are kept occupied by providing a wide range of learning activities to help build resilience and contribute to a pupil's overall well-being. • Prompt response when a pupil goes missing from school by involving parents and mobilising other agencies. • There is close liaison with the local authority where a pupil's behaviour is dangerous, and requires exclusion from school and/or a managed move to another setting.	• All pupils make successful transfers and transitions year on year, from FS to KS1, KS1 to KS2, KS2 to KS3, KS3 to KS4 and KS4 to post-16. • Consideration is given to whether some groups of pupils get excluded more often than others, and finding ways to reduce and address this issue. • A wide range of out-of-school-hours activities, including homework clubs, arts and creative activities, sport and other recreational activities, including play opportunities are on offer. • There is good access to childcare, family learning, parenting support and information.

Source: CDSF 2008b.

Table 4.6 provides a framework for recording evidence of the impact of any additional interventions or support, which can be fed into the Ofsted SEF.

Key stakeholder involvement in evaluating the impact of *ECM* provision

Key stakeholders' participation in judging the quality, effectiveness, strengths, weaknesses and impact of additional provision on improving pupils' *ECM* well-being outcomes is important, in relation to best value and accountability. The key stakeholders comprise of: senior leaders and managers; governors; teachers; teaching assistants; learning mentors; practitioners from external agencies and organisations; and service users, i.e. children and young people, their parents/carers and families. They all have a vital role to play in contributing to the quality assurance process, which checks that appropriate and effective services are provided to meet the needs of the service users. Key stakeholders' involvement in evaluation can be ongoing, i.e. each school term or every six months, or on an annual basis. Those responsible for delivering or commissioning additional provision, advice and support for *Every Child Matters* are more likely to be undertaking more regular checks and balances throughout the year, while pupils, parents/carers and governors may be completing an annual survey as part of the whole school/setting's self-evaluation process.

The best way to involve staff from within the school/setting and external practitioners from services and other organisations is through performance management or appraisal procedures, which set an agreed performance objective related to improving pupils' *ECM* well-being outcomes. This *ECM* objective will be linked to the school/setting or service improvement/development plan *ECM* priorities for the year, which are, in turn, reflected in team, aspect or subject development plans.

Examples of a range of *ECM* evaluation tools for various stakeholders are illustrated in Figures 4.2 to 4.5.

Table 4.6 Evaluating the impact of additional support and interventions of school and/or external agency practitioners

Impact of practitioner support and interventions on improving the Every Child Matters outcomes for pupils

Nature of support and interventions for ECM well-being	Be healthy	Stay safe	Enjoy and achieve	Make a positive contribution	Achieve economic well-being

Practitioner: _____ Date completed: _____

From: Cheminais, Rita, *The Pocket Guide to Every Child Matters*, London: Routledge, © Rita Cheminais 2010.

The headteacher values the views of pupils on how well the school is doing in meeting the five *Every Child Matters* outcomes.

Please answer all the questions and return the survey to your form teacher.

Place a ✓ in the relevant boxes

I am a boy ☐   I am a girl ☐   I am in form/class: _____

QUESTIONS

1 How has the school helped you to be healthy?

healthy meals/ ☐   access to ☐   PE/sports ☐   healthy ☐   an adult ☐
packed   drinking   activities   lifestyle   listener
lunches   water   advice

guidance on ☐   outdoor play ☐   quiet place ☐
relationships/   space/facilities in school
sex education

2 What else could the school do to improve your health and healthy lifestyles?

3 How has the school helped you to be safe and feel safe?

safety signs/ ☐   bullying is ☐   school adult ☐   safety in ☐
rules displayed   dealt with   to go to if I   lessons
                    quickly   don't feel safe   is good

school trips ☐   community ☐
are safe   safety is known

4 What else could the school do to improve your safety and well-being?

5 How has the school helped you to enjoy school and learning, and to achieve?

lessons are ☐   bad behaviour ☐   support for ☐   I have access ☐
interesting/fun   in lessons is   learning is   to ICT in
                  dealt with   available   school

I review ☐   good range ☐
my own   of after-school
learning   activities/clubs

6 How else could the school help you to enjoy school and learning more?

7 How has the school enabled you to make a positive contribution?

pupils' views ☐   pupils inform ☐   there are voluntary, ☐   pupils ☐
are listened to   school decisions   charity and community   contributions
                                            activities for pupils   are valued

8 What else could the school do to ensure you make a positive contribution?

9 How has the school helped you to achieve better economic well-being?

information given ☐   life skills ☐   knowing how   money ☐
about jobs, careers,   are taught   to work with   management
subject options   others   is taught

mini-enterprise ☐   help with ☐
activities exist   moving on to
                         next school/college

10 How else could the school help you to improve your economic well-being?

11 Overall, what else would you like to see happen in school to make the *Every Child Matters* outcomes even better for you and other pupils?

12 Is there anything else you wish to comment on about *Every Child Matters* in school? If yes, please write your comment below.

Thank you for taking part in this school survey.

Figure 4.2 Pupils' *Every Child Matters* survey.

1   What have been your most significant contributions this year to improving pupils *Every Child Matters (ECM)* well-being outcomes?

2   What aspect of your work with pupils has had the greatest impact on improving their *ECM* well-being outcomes?

3   What have been the pupils' views about your teaching and/or support in relation to helping them achieve better *ECM* well-being outcomes?

4   What opportunities have you had to discuss pupils' progress towards achieving good *ECM* well-being outcomes, with other colleagues and practitioners?

5   What have been the barriers, if any, to your *ECM* work with pupils?

6   How could these barriers be removed?

7   Which, if any, aspects of the *ECM* well-being outcomes do you consider requires further development, within the school/setting?

8   Is there any further comment you wish to make about *Every Child Matters*?

Thank you for completing this survey to support school self-evaluation.

Figure 4.3 School staff and multi-agency practitioners *Every Child Matters* survey.

The school values the views of parents/carers on how well the school is improving pupils' *Every Child Matters* well-being outcomes.

Please answer all the questions and return the survey to the school office.

I have a child/children in the following year group(s) _____

QUESTIONS

1   The school has helped my child to be healthy and to lead a healthy lifestyle.
    YES ☐   NO ☐

2. What else could the school do to improve your child's physical health and emotional well-being?

3   The school has helped my child to be safe and well cared for in school.
    YES ☐   NO ☐

4   What else could the school do to improve the safety and welfare of my child?

5   The school has enabled my child to enjoy learning and to achieve at school.
    YES ☐   NO ☐

6   What else could the school do to enable your child to enjoy school and their learning more?

7   The school has enabled my child to make a positive contribution this year.
    YES ☐   NO ☐

8   What else could the school do to increase opportunities for your child to make a positive contribution?

9   The school has helped my child to develop a better understanding about how to achieve economic well-being.
    YES ☐   NO ☐

10 What else could the school do to improve your child's understanding of how to achieve economic well-being?

11 Overall, what would you like to see happen next in school to make the *Every Child Matters* outcomes even better for your child?

12 Is there any further comment you wish to make about the *Every Child Matters* outcomes in the school? If there is, please write your comment below.

Thank you for completing this survey.

Figure 4.4 Parents/carers' *Every Child Matters* survey.

From: Cheminais, Rita, *The Pocket Guide to Every Child Matters*, London: Routledge, © Rita Cheminais 2010

1 How often do you hear about the pupils' progress in the *Every Child Matters* well-being outcomes in the school?

2 How do you get to know the pupils' views about *Every Child Matters* in the school?

3 What are the pupils telling you about the *Every Child Matters* well-being outcomes and provision in the school?

4 What are the school's strengths in the *Every Child Matters* well-being outcomes, and how do you know?

5 What are the school's weaknesses and areas for further development in relation to the *Every Child Matters* well-being outcomes?

6 In your role as a school governor, what more could you do to enable pupils to have a greater say about *Every Child Matters* provision?

7 What really matters to pupils in the school in relation to the *Every Child Matters* well-being outcomes?

8 What has been the value added in relation to improving pupils' *Every Child Matters* well-being outcomes over the last school year?

9 In which *Every Child Matters* outcome(s) does the school achieve best in?

10 Where are the gaps in *Every Child Matters* provision in school?

Thank you for completing this survey to support school self-evaluation

Figure 4.5 School governors' *Every Child Matters* survey.

From: Cheminais, Rita, *The Pocket Guide to Every Child Matters*, London: Routledge, © Rita Cheminais 2010.

Questions for reflection

- How are the pupils you teach, support or work with performing in relation to the school-level indicators for well-being?
- What are the findings from monitoring and evaluating the *ECM* outcomes for the pupils in your class telling you overall?
- Are pupils in your class making sufficient progress in the five *ECM* outcomes? If not, why not, and how will you address this issue?
- What are the strengths and weaknesses of *Every Child Matters* in your classroom?
- Are there any gaps in your *ECM* practice? If so, how do you intend to address the *ECM* gaps?
- How do you intend to feed the impact of your teaching and interventions to improve pupils' *ECM* outcomes into the Ofsted SEF?

5

The *Every Child Matters* team in schools and other education settings

---

This chapter will cover:
- who is likely to be a member of the *ECM* team;
- what we mean by collaborative working;
- what the required knowledge and skills are for collaborative team work to improve *ECM* outcomes for children and young people;
- key principles that promote effective team work.

Members of the *ECM* team

The multi-disciplinary team made up of different practitioners and colleagues from the children's workforce is an important vehicle for delivering improved *ECM* well-being outcomes for children and young people. The size of such a team depends on the complexity of needs of the children and young people within the setting, and on the level of social deprivation prevalent in the local area.

The introduction of extended services delivered in children's centres and schools has also resulted in a wider range of external agencies, services and voluntary and community sector organisations working with more vulnerable children and young people in order to improve their *ECM* outcomes. Together with the teachers, teaching assistants and learning mentors within a school or other educational setting, these external partners can add considerable value, in terms of ensuring better well-being outcomes for children and young people. A school, in particular, cannot be expected to work alone in relation to implementing the *ECM* initiative.

The members of an *ECM* multi-disciplinary team may include: police officers; doctors; nurses; teachers; teaching assistants; learning mentors; education welfare officers; educational psychologists; nursery staff; social workers; therapists; youth workers; leisure and recreational workers; housing staff; and those practitioners who work in criminal/youth justice, mental health or drug and alcohol services.

The Team Around the Child (TAC) is another example of a smaller, sharply focused team, comprising between four and six practitioners from different services, i.e. educational psychologist, social worker, health visitor, speech and language therapist and staff from within the school/setting such as the SENCO, or learning mentor, who come together in response to a child or young person's individual needs to offer support and interventions to the child and family.

Table 5.1 gives an example of the role of some of the key practitioners working in the *ECM* team or the TAC.

What is meant by collaborative working

Collaboration has become the buzz word used in the twenty-first century to describe cooperative joint-partnership working between individuals in an organisation, service or team. Collaboration refers to two or more people working together to address improving children's outcomes. These practitioners may be from within the school's/setting's own staff and/or include children's workforce members from external agencies and organisations.

Collaborative working relies on mutual trust and respect, shared thinking, shared vision, shared goals, shared planning, shared problem solving, shared responsibilities, shared understanding and complementary skills and efforts. Collaboration also involves activities such as two-way communication, information sharing and risk taking. Good collaborative working between practitioners leads to far more efficient and effective practice. The prime aim of collaborative working in any *ECM* team or TAC is to improve outcomes for children and young people by identifying and removing barriers to learning.

Table 5.1 Roles of some key *Every Child Matters* practitioners in schools

Learning mentor	Social care worker	School nurse	Educational psychologist
• Help pupils engage more effectively in learning via individual and small group support • Provide support and interventions to enable pupils to manage their behaviour and emotions, e.g. anger management, conflict resolution, peer mediation • Help to reduce exclusions • Provide direct support and guidance to pupils on study skills, personal organisation, revision and exam techniques • Implement programmes of support to prevent bullying	• Rapid response case work • Parent/carers and family support, e.g. parent drop-ins, family learning classes • Support transition from nursery to primary and from primary to secondary school • Anger management • Support the CAF process • Support the school's PSHE programme • Signposting to specialist services • Counselling and mentoring • Relationship building between schools and families • Group and one-to-one support for children and young people	• Provide confidential advice and guidance on a range of health-related issues including nutrition, exercise, smoking, mental health, drug abuse, sexual health • Promote good health and support children and young people to make healthy life choices • Contribute to the school's PSHE programme and the Healthy Schools initiative • Help to develop and update the school's health and safety policy and the sex education policy • Provide advice on healthy school meals, and access to drinking water for pupils	• Undertake therapeutic work with children and their parents • Early identification of problems and early intervention • Engage in action research to promote increased teacher knowledge of good inclusive practice, and raise expectations • Engage in projects to raise pupil achievement and improve provision for BESD pupils • Support the professional development of teachers, TAs, and contribute to governor training • Work collaboratively with other multi-agency practitioners

Table 5.1 (*Continued*)

• Provide motivational programmes to raise pupils' aspirations, improve their confidence and build their self-esteem and resilience • Work in partnership with multi-agency practitioners such as EWOs to improve attendance • Liaise and work with parents; deliver workshops on parenting skills, family learning and managing their child's behaviour • Run breakfast clubs and homework clubs • Support pupil transitions • Support and train pupil mentors • Support and assist school staff in dealing with difficult pupil incidents	• Pupil support for bereavement, self-esteem, behaviour and attendance, depression, self-harming, school anxiety/phobia, family violence, substance abuse, bullying, suicidal threats • Act as an advocate for children, young people and their families • Deliver workshops and seminars to teachers and other school staff, related to social-emotional and risk issues such as: how to manage pupils' behaviour in the classroom • Help to identify school staff and other agency practitioners who can help to maximise pupil success	• Contribute to the school's extended services provision by running an after-school healthy-eating cookery club • Provide a drop-in clinic for children, young people and their parents on, or near the school site • Support individual pupils with long-term medical needs health plans • Support the safeguarding work of the school by advising staff • Provide immunisation to pupils, where appropriate • Run parent groups	• Support parents/carers as key partners in their child's leaning and well-being • Promote a solution-oriented approach to problem solving in relation to pupil learning, behaviour and well-being • Work with individual children and young people who have severe, complex and challenging needs • Involvement in the statutory assessment of children with the most complex needs, e.g. SEN • Monitor and evaluate the impact of EP interventions and training on improving pupils *ECM* outcomes

Table 5.1 (*Continued*)

Education welfare officer	Art therapist	Police officer	Housing officer
• Support schools in improving pupils' attendance • Undertake targeted individual and group case work • Protect children from the risks of exploitation and harm, e.g. child employment • Involved in school-based attendance projects • Provide consultation and advice to schools on attendance strategy and individual cases • Liaise with Home Education and Out of School Learning Services • Monitors the licensing of child employment and child entertainment in the local area	• Use art materials and artwork to enable troubled pupils to communicate their feelings and problems • Facilitate non-verbal and verbal communication through creative art work for pupils • Keep written records of work undertaken and review art therapy work undertaken with targeted pupils • Liaise with other practitioners such as teachers, TAs, social workers, CAMHS workers, educational psychologists • Keep parents/carers informed about the type of art therapy work being undertaken with their child	• Help to reduce truancy and exclusions • Helps to reduce victimisation, criminality and anti-social behaviour within the school and its community • Help to identify and work with children and young people at risk of becoming victims of crime and bullying, or offenders • Support school staff in dealing with incidents of crime, victimisation or anti-social behaviour • Promotes the full participation of children and young people in the life of the school and its wider community	• Help to reduce anti-social behaviour among young people in the community by contributing to providing youth activities • Provide funding, buildings and land for youth, community and environmental projects • Help to build greater understanding between the old and the young in the community through joint local history projects • Work in close collaboration with other services, e.g. police, youth service to inform provision for young people in the community

Table 5.1 (*Continued*)

• Provide professional advice and support to schools and education staff on safeguarding arrangements, including child protection • Take a lead role in allegations against members of staff and volunteers • Provide training to schools, governors and education staff, e.g. INSET, coaching and mentoring • Support and advise parents to ensure they fulfil their statutory responsibilities with respect to the education of their children • Involvement in any court action where parents/carers are being prosecuted for their child's non-attendance at school	• Run parent skills workshops to help parents/carers to support their child while in therapy • Contributes to the school's SEAL programme, where appropriate	• Provide educational inputs for pupils in the classroom on aspects of citizenship and personal safety as part of PSHE, e.g. covering topics such as drugs, alcohol and bullying • Work in partnership with other agencies such as the Youth Offending Team (YOT), Youth Justice and Connexions. • Build positive relationships between the police and young people	• Consult with children and young people on the facilities and services they want in the local community • Provide inputs to the school curriculum on housing education and homelessness • Help school staff to prepare pupils for leaving home and finding a home on their own • Provide information and advice to young people on housing choices, housing benefits, getting a mortgage and how to choose the right property • Advise school staff on how to support the learning of pupils who are living in temporary accommodation

The required knowledge and skills required for collaborative working

All children's workforce practitioners from public, private and voluntary sector services have to meet the common core of skills and knowledge required for effective multi-agency collaborative working. Table 5.2 provides an overview of the six areas of expertise in the common core of skills and knowledge.

There also exists a joint statement of inter-professional values and dispositions, produced in 2007 by the General Social Care Council (GSCC), the General Teaching Council for England (GTC) and the Nursing and Midwifery Council (NMC), which states:

- Children's practitioners value the contribution that a range of colleagues make to children's lives, and they form effective relationships across the children's workforce. Their inter-professional practice is based on a willingness to bring their own expertise to bear on the pursuit of shared goals for children, and a respect for the expertise of others. Practitioners recognise that children and families, and colleagues value transparency and reliability, and strive to make sure that processes, roles, goals and resources are clear.
- Practitioners involved in inter-professional work recognise the need to be clear about lines of communication, management and accountability as these may be more complex than in their specialist setting.
- They uphold the standards and values of their own professionals in their inter-professional work. They understand that sharing responsibility for children's outcomes does not mean acting beyond their competence or responsibilities.
- They are committed to taking action if safety or standards are compromised, whether that means alerting their own manager/ employer or another appropriate authority.
- Children's practitioners understand that the knowledge, understanding and skills for inter-professional work may differ from those in their own specialism and they are committed to professional learning in their area as well as in their own field, through training and engagement with research and other evidence.

Table 5.2 Common core of skills and knowledge for multi-agency working

Skills	Knowledge
Communication and teamwork • Communicate effectively with other practitioners and professionals by listening and ensuring that you are being listened to. • Appreciate that others may not have the same understanding of professional terms and may interpret abbreviations such as acronyms differently. • Provide timely, appropriate, succinct information to enable other practitioners to deliver their support to the child or young person, parent or carer. • Record, summarise, share and feed back information, using IT skills where necessary to do so. • Work in a team context, forging and sustaining relationships across agencies and respecting the contribution of others working with children, young people and families. • Share experience through formal and informal exchanges and work with adults who are parents/carers. **Assertiveness** • Be proactive, initiate necessary action and be able and prepared to put forward your own judgements. • Have the confidence to challenge situations by looking beyond your immediate role and asking considered questions. • Present facts and judgements objectively.	**Your role and remit** • Know your main job and responsibilities within your working environment. • Know the value and expertise you bring to a team and that brought by your colleagues. **Know how to make queries** • Know your role within different group situations and how you contribute to the overall group process, understanding the value of sharing how you approach your role with other professionals. • Develop your skills and knowledge with training from experts, to minimise the need for referral to specialist services, enabling continuity for the family, child or young person while enhancing your own skills and knowledge. • Have general knowledge and understanding of the range of organisations and individuals working with children, young people and those caring for them, and be aware of the roles and responsibilities of other professionals. **Procedures and working methods** • Know what to do in given cases, e.g. for referrals or raising concerns. • Know what the triggers are for reporting incidents or unexpected behaviour.

Table 5.2 (*Continued*)

- Identify possible sources of support within your own working environment.
- Judge when you should provide the support yourself and when you should refer the situation to another practitioner or professional.

- Know how to work within your own and other organisational values, beliefs and cultures.
- Know what to do when there is an insufficient response from other organisations or agencies, while maintaining a focus on what is in the child or young person's best interests.
- Understand the way that partner services operate – their procedures, objectives, role and relationships – in order to be able to work effectively alongside them.
- Know about the Common Assessment Framework for Children and Young People (CAF) and, where appropriate, how to use it.

The law, policies and procedures
- Know about the existence of key laws relating to children and young people and where to obtain further information.
- Know about employers' safeguarding and health and safety policies and procedures, and how they apply in the wider working environment.

Source: HM Government 2005: 18–20

- They are committed to reflecting on and improving their inter-professional practice, and to apply their inter-professional learning to their specialist work with children.
- Work with children can be emotionally demanding, and children's practitioners are sensitive to and supportive of each others' well-being.

(Source: Nursing Midwifery Council, General Social Care Council and the General Teaching Council for England 2007)

Professional standards for teachers and collaborative working

The TDA in 2007 revised the national professional standards for teachers to reflect the five *ECM* outcomes and the children's workforce six areas of the common core of skills and knowledge.

Table 5.3 provides an overview of the relevant Qualified Teacher Status (QTS) and the core professional standards for all teachers which relate to inter-professional working. The professional standards use the term 'colleagues' to refer to all those professionals with whom a teacher might work, for example, other teaching colleagues and the wider workforce in the educational setting such as teaching assistants, learning mentors, midday supervisors, as well as other practitioners from external agencies such as educational psychologists, speech and language therapists, police and physiotherapists.

The National Occupational Standards for supporting teaching and learning

In June 2007 the TDA published the national occupational standards (NOS) for supporting teaching and learning, which related to teaching assistants and members of the school's/educational setting's children's workforce, other than teachers, who support teaching and learning.

The NOS provide competence statements relating to the skills and knowledge required to support teaching and learning not only in schools but in other educational settings such as Academies, PRUs and learning centres. The national occupational standards cover working with colleagues as one of the five key areas of responsibility. Table 5.4 outlines the relevant key national occupational standards which are relevant to collaborative working.

Table 5.3 Professional standards for teachers and multi-professional working

Qualified Teacher Status (QTS)	*All teachers – Core*
Professional attributes **Communicating and working with others** Q4. Communicate effectively with children, young people, colleagues, parents and carers. Q5. Recognise and respect the contribution that colleagues, parents and carers can make to the development and well-being of children and young people, and to raising the levels of attainment. Q6. Have a commitment to collaboration and cooperative working. **Professional knowledge and understanding** **Achievement and diversity** Q20. Know and understand the roles of colleagues with specific responsibilities, including those with responsibility for learners with special educational needs and disabilities and other individual learning needs.	**Professional attributes** **Communicating and working with others** C4(a). Communicate effectively with children, young people and colleagues. C5. Recognise and respect the contributions that colleagues, parents and carers can make to the development and well-being of children and young people, and to raising their levels of attainment. C6. Have a commitment to collaboration and cooperative working where appropriate. **Professional knowledge and understanding** **Achievement and diversity** C20. Understand the roles of colleagues such as those having specific responsibilities for learners with special educational needs, disabilities and other individual learning needs, and the contributions they can make to the learning, development and well-being of children and young people. C21. Know when to draw on the expertise of colleagues, such as those with responsibility for the safeguarding of children and young people with special educational needs and disabilities, and to refer to sources of information, advice and support from external agencies.

Table 5.3 (*Continued*)

Health and well-being Q21(b). Know how to identify and support children and young people whose progress, development or well-being is affected by changes or difficulties in their personal circumstances, and when to refer them to colleagues for specialist support. **Professional skills** **Team working and collaboration** Q32. Work as a team member and identify opportunities for working with colleagues, sharing the development of effective practice with them. Q33. Ensure that colleagues working with them are appropriately involved in supporting learning and understand the roles they are expected to fulfil.	**Health and well-being** C25. Know how to identify and support children and young people whose progress, development or well-being is affected by changes or difficulties in their personal circumstances, and when to refer them to colleagues for specialist support. **Professional skills** **Team working and collaboration** C40. Work as a team member and identify opportunities for working with colleagues, managing their work where appropriate and sharing the development of effective practice with them. C41. Ensure that colleagues working with them are appropriately involved in supporting learning and understand the roles they are expected to fulfil.

Source: TDA 2007b.

Table 5.4 National occupational standards for supporting teaching and learning in schools: working with colleagues

Unit number	Unit description
STL4	**Contribute to positive relationships** – with children, young people and adults, valuing people equally.
STL5	**Provide effective support for your colleagues** – contributing to effective teamwork and maintaining working relationships with colleagues.
STL20	**Develop and promote positive relationships** – communicate with adults, children and young people.
STL21	**Support the development and effectiveness of work teams** – by being an effective member of a work team contributing to effective team practice.
STL60	**Liaise with parents, carers and families** – facilitating information sharing while ensuring professional integrity in communications with parents, carers and families.
STL62	**Develop and maintain working relationships with other practitioners** – doing what you can to support other practitioners' work, utilising your strengths and expertise in partnership working.
STL63	**Provide leadership for your team** – provide direction to team members, and motivate and support them to achieve the teams' and their own personal objectives. Allocate and check work in the team.
STL64	**Provide leadership in your area of responsibility** – providing direction to colleagues in a specific programme, initiative or policy, motivating and supporting them to achieve the vision and objectives for the area.
STL65	**Allocate and check work in your team** – fair and effective allocation of work to team members, checking on progress and quality of the teams' work.
STL66	**Lead and motivate volunteers** – briefing volunteers on their responsibilities and requirements, helping them to resolve any problems during volunteering activities, giving them feedback on their work, and respecting their needs and preferences.
STL67	**Provide learning opportunities for colleagues** – support colleagues in identifying their learning needs and provide opportunities to address these needs. Encourage colleagues to take responsibility for their own learning wherever possible.
STL68	**Support learners by mentoring in the workplace** – plan the mentoring process, set up and maintain the mentoring relationship and provide mentoring to colleagues and trainees in the workplace.
STL69	**Support competence achieved in the workplace** – assess staff performance in the workplace against agreed standards, and give them feedback on their performance.

Source: TDA 2007a.

Key principles for effective collaborative working

The following principles enable effective collaborative working to take place:

- The respective roles and responsibilities of all members of the *ECM* team or the TAC are clear and understood by teaching staff, TAs and members of the respective multi-agency team(s).
- Protocols and procedures for referring children and young people on to agencies and services are clear.
- All collaborative partnership working between school staff and those from external agencies is based on agreed goals, shared values, trust and mutual respect.
- Good effective two-way communication exists between practitioners/colleagues for information sharing.
- Opportunities exist for joint inter-professional training and development.
- Realistic expectations exist as to what the collaborative partnership can hope to achieve.
- Members of the *ECM*/TAC team have quality time to meet at regular intervals to review progress in improving children and young people's well-being outcomes, and to plan for future improvements.
- Clear procedures exist for the joint monitoring and evaluation of the impact of additional support, provision and interventions in improving children and young people's *ECM* outcomes.

Questions for reflection

- How many pupils in your class are receiving additional support and interventions from external agencies and school learning-support staff?
- Which multi-agency practitioners are working with those pupils who have additional needs?
- How are you using the information from external practitioners about how best to meet the needs of more vulnerable pupils in your class?
- Have there been any barriers that have impeded your collaborative working practice with learning-support staff and external practitioners? If so, how could the barriers be removed?
- What has worked well for you in relation to collaborative working with other staff in school, and with external practitioners?
- How do you know that the impact of collaborative working practice has helped to improve the *ECM* outcomes for pupils in your class?

Every Child Matters Jargon Buster

Additional needs – describes all children and young people at risk of poor *ECM* outcomes, who require extra support from education, health or social services for a limited time, or on a longer-term basis.

At risk – is a term used to describe a child or young person believed and thought to be at risk of significant harm, social exclusion or offending, who requires protection from the local authority and services/agencies.

Child – is a person under the age of 18. The term 'children and young people' is also used as a catch-all phrase to cover this age group.

Children's Centre – is a Sure Start one-stop shop and community service hub for parents/carers and children under five, offering early education and childcare, family support, health services, employment advice and specialist support on a single site to improve their life chances.

Children's Trusts – bring together all services for children and young people in an area in order to improve outcomes.

Common Assessment Framework – is a holistic assessment tool used by the children's workforce to assess the additional needs of children and young people at the first sign of difficulties.

ContactPoint – is a quick way to find out who else is working with the same child or young person, making it easier to deliver more coordinated support.

Every Child Matters – is a government initiative and strategy aimed at protecting, nurturing and improving the life chances and well-being outcomes of all children and young people, particularly those who are disadvantaged or vulnerable.

Extended school – offers a range of core universal services and activities, often beyond the school day, to help meet the needs of children, young people and their families, and the wider community.

Information sharing – is the passing on of relevant information to other agencies, organisations and to individual practitioners that require it in order to deliver better services to children and young people.

Key worker – refers to a practitioner from health, social services or education who provides a lead support and advocacy role to children and young people with more complex needs.

Lead professional – is a designated professional from health, education or social services, who has day-to-day contact with a child or young person, and who coordinates and monitors service provision, acting as a gatekeeper for information sharing.

Looked-after child – refers to any child or young person who is in the care of the local authority, or who is provided with accommodation by the local authority social services department for a continuous period of more than 24 hours. The term also covers children and young people subject to accommodation under a voluntarily agreed series of short-term placements like short breaks, family link placements or respite care.

Multi-agency working – is where those from more than one agency or service work together, sharing aims, information, tasks and responsibilities.

National Service Framework – offers a set of quality standards for health, social care and some education services, which are aimed at reducing inequalities in service provision in order to improve the lives of children/young people.

Outcomes – are identifiable (positive and negative) impacts of interventions and services on children and young people. It also refers to the five *Every Child Matters* outcomes of: be healthy; stay safe; enjoy and achieve; make a positive contribution; and achieve economic well-being.

Personalisation – is where children, young people and their families, as responsible service users, are active participants in the shaping, development and delivery of personalised (tailored and customised) services.

Personalised learning – entails enabling children and young people to achieve their personal best, through working in a way that suits them. It embraces every aspect which includes teaching and learning strategies; ICT; curriculum choice, organisation and timetabling; assessment arrangements; and relationships with the local community.

Practitioners – refers to anyone who works directly with children and young people and their families, whose primary role is to use a particular expertise or professional skill to help promote and improve children and young people's well-being.

Safeguarding – is the process of identifying children and young people who have suffered, or who are likely to suffer, significant harm, and then to take the appropriate action, in accordance with the government's guidance on Safeguarding Children in Education (2007), in order to keep them safe.

Specialist services – include child protection services, adoption and fostering services for looked-after children and their families, residential services, and services for children and young people with serious mental health problems such as eating disorders. These services are provided specifically for children and young people with acute or high-level needs who would otherwise be at a high risk of achieving poor outcomes.

Targeted services – provide support for children and young people less likely to achieve optimal outcomes who have additional needs, or complex needs, ideally within universal settings such as Children's Centres and full-service extended schools.

Team Around the Child – is an individualised, personalised and evolving team of a few different practitioners, who come together to provide practical support to help an individual child.

Universal services – also known as mainstream services, are provided and made routinely available to all children and young people and their families, which includes Early Years provision, mainstream schools and Connexions, general practitioner (GP), midwives and health visitors.

Vulnerable children and young people – refers to those at risk of social exclusion, who are disadvantaged and whose life chances are at risk. It includes those in public care; children with learning difficulties and disabilities; travellers; asylum seekers; excluded pupils; truants; young offenders; young family carers; and children experiencing family stress or affected by domestic violence.

Welfare – refers to child-safety issues and child protection.

Well-being – refers to having the basic things you need to live and be healthy, safe and happy. It also refers to the five *Every Child Matters* well-being outcomes.

Young person – is someone aged 14 to 17 years. It also refers to those aged 18 to 25 years.

Useful websites

www.dcsf.gov.uk
www.everychildmatters.gov.uk
www.ncsl.org.uk/*ECM*
www.ofsted.gov.uk
www.qca.org.uk/curriculum
www.qca.org.uk/qca_15299.aspx
www.standards.dcsf.gov.uk/personalisedlearning
www.standards.dcsf.gov.uk/innovation-unit/personalisation
www.tda.gov.uk
www.teachernet.gov.uk
www.teachers.tv

References and further reading

Chamberlain, T., Lewis, K., Teeman, D. and Kendall, L. (2006) *Annual Survey of Trends in Education 2006: Schools' Concerns and Their Implications for Local Authorities* (LGA Report 5/06). Slough: NFER.

Cheminais, R. (2008) *Every Child Matters: A Practical Guide for Teaching Assistants*. London: Routledge.

Cheminais, R. (2009) *Effective Multi-Agency Partnerships: Putting Every Child Matters into Practice*. London: SAGE Publications.

DCSF (2008a) *Evaluating Every Child Matters: The SIP's Role in Engaging the School*. Nottingham: Department for Children, Schools and Families.

DCSF (2008b) *Schools' Role in Promoting Pupil Well Being: Draft Guidance for Consultation*. London: Department for Children, Schools and Families.

DfES (2003) *Every Child Matters*. London: The Stationery Office.

DfES (2004) *Every Child Matters: Change for Children in Schools*. Nottingham: Department for Education and Skills.

DfES (2006) *Safeguarding Children and Safer Recruitment in Education*. Nottingham: Department for Education and Skills.

DfES (2007) *An Investigation of Personalised Learning Approaches used by Schools*. Research Report No. 843. Nottingham: University of Sussex/Department for Education and Skills.

DfES/DH (2004) *National Service Framework for Children, Young People and Maternity Services: Executive Summary*. London: Department for Education and Skills/Department of Health.

Fullan, M. (2002) The Change Leader. *Educational Leadership*, May 2002. EBSCO Publishing.

GTC (2007a) HM Government: Children's Workforce Strategy Update – Spring 2007. *Building a World-Class Workforce for Children, Young People and Families*. London: General Teaching Council for England.

GTC (2007b) *Inter-professional Values Underpinning Work with Children and Young People. Joint Statement*. London: General Teaching Council for England.

Harris, A., Allen, T. and Goodall, J. (2007) *Understanding the Reasons Why Schools Do or Do Not Fully Engage with the ECM/ ES Agenda*. Nottingham: National College for School Leadership and the Training and Development Agency for Schools.

Her Majesty's Government (2005) *Common Core of Skills and Knowledge for the Children's Workforce*. London: Department for Education and Skills.

Last, G. (2004) *Personalised Learning: Adding Value to the Learning Journey through the Primary School*. London: Department for Education and Skills.

Lewis, K., Chamberlain, T., Riggall, A., Gagg, K. and Rudd, P. (2007) *Annual Survey of Trends in Education 2007: Schools' Concerns and Their Implications for Local Authorities* (LGA Report 4/07). Slough: NFER.

NCSL (2002/2003) Leading and Managing Staff. NPQH Development Module 3, D1, Strategic Direction and Development of the School, Change and the Individual. Nottingham: National College for School Leadership.

NFER (2006) *How is the Every Child Matters Agenda Affecting Schools? Annual Survey of Trends in Education 2006*. Slough: National Foundation for Educational Research.

NFER (2008) *How is the Every Child Matters Agenda Affecting Schools? Annual Survey of Trends in Education 2007*. Slough: National Foundation for Educational Research.

Ofsted (2005) *Every Child Matters: Framework for the Inspection of Schools*. London: Office for Standards in Education.

Ofsted (2006a) *Using the Evaluation Schedule: Guidance for Inspectors of Schools*. London: Office for Standards in Education.

Ofsted (2006b) *Healthy Schools, Healthy Children? The Contribution of Education to Pupils' Health and Well-being*. HMI 2563. London: Office for Standards in Education.

Ofsted (2007) *Self-Evaluation Form for Primary Schools (With and Without Nursery Provision), Middle Schools (Deemed Primary)*. London: Office for Standards in Education, Children's Services and Skills.

Ofsted (2008a) *How Well Are They Doing? The Impact of Children's Centres and Extended Schools*. London: Office for Standards in Education, Children's Services and Skills.

Ofsted (2008b) *Using Data, Improving Schools*. London: Office for Standards in Education, Children's Services and Skills.

Ofsted (2008c) *A Focus on Improvement: Proposals for Maintained School Inspections from September 2009*. London: Office for Standards in Education, Children's Services and Skills.

Ofsted (2008d) *Indicators of a School's Contribution to Well Being. Consultation Document*. London: Office for Standards in Education, Children's Services and Skills.

Ofsted (2008e) *TellUs3 Survey*. London: Office for Standards in Education, Children's Services and Skills.

QCA (2008) *Every Child Matters at the Heart of the Curriculum*. London: Qualifications and Curriculum Authority.

TDA (2007a) *National Occupational Standards for Supporting Teaching and Learning in Schools*. London: Training and Development Agency for Schools.

TDA (2007b) *Professional Standards for Teachers: Why Sit Still in Your Career?* London: Training and Development Agency for Schools.

TDA (2007c) *What Is Every Child Matters?* London: Training and Development Agency for Schools.

Index